FDI Qualities Review of Chile

BOOSTING SUSTAINABLE DEVELOPMENT AND DIVERSIFICATION

OECD
BETTER POLICIES FOR BETTER LIVES

Please cite this publication as:
OECD (2023), *FDI Qualities Review of Chile: Boosting Sustainable Development and Diversification*, OECD Publishing, Paris, https://doi.org/10.1787/98bf1829-en.

ISBN 978-92-64-32988-1 (print)
ISBN 978-92-64-62426-9 (pdf)
ISBN 978-92-64-39855-9 (HTML)
ISBN 978-92-64-75332-7 (epub)

Photo credits: Cover © leonardospencer/Getty Images.

Corrigenda to OECD publications may be found on line at: www.oecd.org/about/publishing/corrigenda.htm.

Foreword

This *FDI Qualities Review of Chile* examines how foreign direct investment (FDI) supports sustainable development in Chile and provides guidance on how to enhance its positive contribution. It offers an analysis of how FDI has contributed to national sustainable development goals in Chile and examines the potential and benefits of diversifying the FDI landscape towards more sustainable activities. The review also provides a detailed analysis of the policy and regulatory framework that influences the sustainable development impact of FDI. The report compares Chile with other OECD economies and provides examples of good practices based on the experience of other countries.

The report comprises three chapters. Chapter 1 provides an overview of the main challenges and opportunities for sustainable development in Chile and presents a summary of the main findings of the study, which show the role that FDI currently plays in supporting sustainable development. Based on an assessment of Chile's regulatory and policy framework, it also derives overarching policy considerations to strengthen the benefits of foreign investment. Chapter 2 examines in depth the impact of FDI on trade and GVC integration; productivity and innovation; job quality and skills development; and the low-carbon transition. It also discusses how attracting FDI in a wider range of sectors can help improve the economic diversification of the Chilean economy. Chapter 3 assesses the policy and regulatory framework influencing the impact of FDI on sustainable development, with a focus on productivity, innovation, skills development and low-carbon transition.

The review has been prepared by the OECD in close co-ordination with InvestChile and the Ministry of Foreign Affairs' Undersecretariat for International Economic Relations (SUBREI). It will help Chile decide where to focus its investment attraction and facilitation efforts to become a more diversified, resilient and knowledge-based economy. It can ensure that FDI supports sustainable and inclusive growth after the COVID-19 outbreak and economic recession. This review is part of a series of *FDI Qualities Reviews*, supporting the implementation of the *OECD Council Recommendation on FDI Qualities,* adopted by OECD Ministers in 2022.

This review was prepared by Letizia Montinari and Stratos Kamenis of the Investment Division in the OECD Directorate for Financial and Enterprise Affairs, under the overall guidance of Ana Novik, Head of the Investment Division and Martin Wermelinger, Head of Investment Qualities and Incentives Unit. Alejandro Buvinic Alarcon, Head of Services, Investment and Digital Economy Division at SUBREI, was instrumental in providing guidance and feedback to the OECD team. Mertol Ozaltan and Raimundo Smith provided substantive inputs. The report benefited from discussions with and comments from Al Hussami Fares, Alexandre de Crombrugghe, Juan Pablo Candia, Iris Mantovani, Rodrigo Monardes, Francisco Picón Gutiérrez, Alejandro Riquelme, Monika Sztajerowska, and Stephen Thomsen.

Table of contents

FIGURES

TABLES

Follow OECD Publications on:

https://twitter.com/OECD

https://www.facebook.com/theOECD

https://www.linkedin.com/company/organisation-eco-cooperation-development-organisation-cooperation-developpement-eco/

https://www.youtube.com/user/OECDiLibrary

https://www.oecd.org/newsletters/

Abbreviations and acronyms

ANID	National Agency for Research and Development
BITs	Bilateral Investment Treaties
CORFO	Corporación de Fomento de la Producción
CRM	Customer relationship management
EU	European Union
KPIs	Key performance indicators
FIA	Foundation for Agricultural Innovation
FDI	Foreign direct investment
FDIRR	FDI Regulatory Restrictiveness index
FTAs	Free Trade Agreements
GDP	Gross domestic product
GVC	Global value chains
IAPMEI	Portuguese SME Competitiveness and Innovation Agency
ICT	Information and Communications Technologies
IIAs	International investment agreements
ILO	International Labour Organization
IPA	Investment promotion agency
LAC	Latin America and the Caribbean
M&A	Merger and acquisition
M&E	Monitoring and evaluation
MNE	Multinational enterprise
MOU	Memorandum of understanding
OECD	Organisation for Economic Co-operation and Development
PPA	Power purchasing agreement
PPP	Public-private partnership
R&D	Research & Development
RBC	Responsible business contact
SDG	Sustainable Development Goal
SENCE	National Training and Employment Service
SME	Small- and medium-sized enterprise
UTM	Unitad Tributaria Mensual

Executive summary

Chile has made impressive strides in terms of economic growth and living standards in recent decades. Yet, the country faces new and important sustainable development challenges. These include first and foremost stimulating productivity growth to sustain continuous improvements in the living standards of its citizens, reducing social inequalities and combating climate change. The 2019-20 social protest and the COVID-19 pandemic have made these challenges yet more pressing and addressing them will be crucial for Chile to become a more prosperous, equitable and resilient economy.

As a small, open economy rich in natural resources, Chile relies heavily on trade and FDI to sustain its economic growth. The importance of FDI for the Chilean economy has increased over time, as evidenced by the growing share of inward FDI stock in GDP, reaching almost 100% in 2020. However, FDI flows to Chile have decreased since 2012, in line with the global trend. Almost 30% of FDI stock is concentrated in finance, renewable energy, trade and medium- and low-tech manufacturing. Geographically, FDI is concentrated in the mining-rich regions of Antofagasta and Atacama and in the capital Santiago. Investors from Europe (the Netherlands, the United Kingdom, Spain and Italy) and North America are the main sources of FDI in Chile. Over the past five years, a significant amount of FDI flows have also come from China, although Chinese FDI is still marginal in the Chilean FDI landscape.

Foreign firms established locally contribute significantly to sustainable development in Chile. They are responsible for more than half of total exports in most sectors, including knowledge-intensive sectors. Moreover, they participate extensively in domestic value chains, as they source their inputs mainly from the domestic market, especially from Chilean SMEs, and sell their production mainly in the domestic market, especially to Chilean SMEs. Sectors with a high concentration of FDI (mining, energy, finance) are more productive and capital-intensive, but contribute less to R&D and have lower job creation potential than other sectors. In most sectors, foreign firms are, on average, more productive and engage more in R&D activities than domestic firms. They also create better paid and higher skilled jobs, including for women. Foreign companies also support Chile's transition to clean energy. They are on average more energy-efficient than Chilean companies and invest considerably in renewable energy (around 90% of FDI in the energy sector goes to renewable energy).

The positive contribution of FDI to sustainable development suggests that foreign firms can play an important role in helping Chile diversify its economy and become a knowledge-intensive economy. Economic activity in Chile is highly focused in services (professional services, trade, and public sector), medium- and low-tech manufacturing, and natural resources. Although these sectors have supported economic growth in Chile in the past decades, they now offer fewer prospects in terms of sustainable development. They contribute less to innovation, productivity growth, quality job creation and low carbon transition. FDI can help Chile develop new competitive edges in knowledge-intensive and green sectors, bringing in new and cleaner technologies and acting as a gateway to international markets.

The quality of the legal and regulatory environment plays a key role in ensuring that FDI supports sustainable development. Overall, Chile's economy is open to FDI. Investment-related policies are non-discriminatory and foreign-owned companies are provided with national treatment. Although Chile has a competition-friendly regulatory environment, a few 'behind-the-border' regulations affect market access conditions in several sectors where foreign firms operate. These include complex regulatory procedures, particularly for large investment projects in strategic sectors, and barriers to public procurement for foreign suppliers of goods and services. As Chile seeks to diversify the type of FDI it attracts, it will be important to improve regulatory procedures and remove barriers to public procurement for foreign companies. Efforts should also be made to mainstream sustainability considerations into Chile's international investment agreements (IIAs). Labour and environmental standards are increasingly part of free trade agreements (FTAs) negotiated by the Ministry of Foreign Affairs; however, more could be done to update "old generation" agreements that do not include sustainable development provisions and strengthen their effective implementation.

In recent years, InvestChile, Chile's investment promotion agency, has prioritised low-carbon and knowledge-intensive FDI. Although new initiatives have been set up to improve the quality of investment promotion services offered to foreign MNEs, monitoring and measuring the contribution of these activities to the Sustainable Development Goals (SDGs) is an area where further progress could be made. InvestChile's representation abroad could also be strengthened to generate contacts and investment projects that contribute to sustainable development, including by establishing overseas offices and strengthening co-ordination with ProChile, the agency in charge of promoting Chile's exports, and the Ministry of Foreign Affairs. The investment promotion action plans to be developed by InvestChile in early 2023 provide a good opportunity to strengthen inter-institutional co-ordination mechanisms for the implementation of the new national strategy on FDI promotion.

In addition, both direct and indirect financial support to knowledge-intensive investments could be better co-ordinated and targeted in order to promote Chile's strategic development priorities in the area of sustainable development and FDI diversification. Chile provides one of the lowest levels of total government support for business R&D among OECD and partner economies. The Government of Chile could consider ways to streamline and consolidate its financial incentives framework, including by strengthening co-ordination and the joint management of the incentives system through the Inter-Ministerial Committee for Sustainable Productive Development, or by leveraging the potential of a new public development bank or the already established Banco del Estado. These reforms should aim to make available a variety of funding instruments and network-building initiatives to crowd-in private investors, including foreign.

Foreign companies operating in Chile should be further incentivised to undertake training activities for their employees and local suppliers. Currently, skills development programmes are implemented by various governmental actors and are not sufficiently aligned with labour market needs. InvestChile should co-ordinate with SENCE, CORFO and Chile's labour intermediation offices to develop joint programmes that enable foreign companies to find the skills they need. The agency could also further promote sectors and activities in line with the existing skills base and provide investors with adequate information on labour market characteristics.

Creating a favourable environment for low-carbon investments is an important political priority for the Chilean Government. Chile's long-term goal of reaching 100% zero-emission electricity generation and 80% renewable energy by 2050 will require a sustained pace of investment in clean energy. Achieving this target should entail targeted policies, in particular for hard-to-abate sectors, and to attract private investment, including FDI, in emerging industries (e.g. green hydrogen). To this end, the current carbon pricing framework should be revised with the aim of raising carbon taxes to levels comparable to international standards and improving their sectoral coverage.

1 Overview and key policy considerations

This chapter provides an overview of the main challenges and opportunities for sustainable development in Chile, and presents a summary of the main findings of the study, which show the role that foreign direct investment currently plays in supporting trade and GVC integration, productivity and innovation, job quality and skills, gender equality and the low-carbon transition. Based on an assessment of Chile's regulatory and policy framework, the chapter also derives overarching policy considerations to strengthen the economic, social and environmental benefits of foreign investment.

Policy considerations

- Continue policy efforts to diversify the economy and shift to knowledge-intensive and green activities will be crucial for Chile to address pressing sustainable development challenges, including stimulating productivity growth to support the continued improvement of living standards of its citizens, reducing social inequalities and combating climate change. Attracting FDI in a broader spectrum of sectors can help Chile achieve a higher level of economic sophistication and become a more prosperous, equitable and resilient economy.
- Streamline sectoral licensing requirements for high-tech manufacturing and knowledge-intensive services, including by digitalising compliance processes related to setting up a business, acquiring permits and undertaking investments in strategic sectors of the economy.
- Remove barriers to foreign supplier participation in public procurement and integrate environmental and social criteria into public tenders as well as clearly defined rules to avoid discretionary decisions.
- Continue efforts to integrate sustainability considerations into Chile's international trade and investment agreements.
- Strengthen InvestChile's capacity to target high value-added investments (e.g. through incentives) and measure the contribution of investment promotion activities to the SDGs and sustainability more generally.
- Consider ways to strengthen InvestChile's investment promotion activities in key markets abroad, including by establishing overseas offices and strengthening co-ordination with ProChile and the Ministry of Foreign Affairs.
- Specify policy co-ordination mechanisms and monitoring and evaluation (M&E) tools for the implementation of the National Strategy for the Promotion of Foreign Investment.
- Adjust the R&D tax incentive scheme to make it more attractive for foreign and domestic firms that seek to engage in innovation-based partnerships.
- Consider ways to streamline and consolidate Chile's investment incentives framework to support the financing of low-carbon and technology-intensive investments, including through enhanced co-ordination and joint management of the incentives system or through new funding tools by CORFO or the Banco del Estado.
- Implement FDI-SME linkage programmes and provide technical assistance to domestic firms, in particular SMEs, to help them become successful suppliers and partners of foreign investors.
- Incentivise foreign MNEs to undertake training activities for their employees and local suppliers, by encouraging greater levels of permanent employment and allowing firms to tailor skills development programmes to the needs of their employees.
- Continue policy efforts to create an enabling environment for renewable energy investments by removing regulatory barriers, providing specific incentives, and reforming the current carbon pricing framework.
- Explore measures to attract investment in the emerging green hydrogen industry – while taking into consideration the early technological maturity of hydrogen technologies and the high risks involved – including through public-private partnerships, incentives for investments in enabling infrastructure, capacity building and training programmes, R&D collaborations and regulation addressing demand-side bottlenecks.

1.1. Main challenges and opportunities for sustainable development in Chile

1.1.1. Low productivity, labour market imbalances and environmental risks are the main challenges to sustainable development in Chile

In recent decades, Chile has experienced significant economic growth that has helped to improve the living standards of its citizens and reduce poverty (Figure 1.1). As a small, open economy rich in natural resources, Chile relies heavily on trade and foreign direct investment (FDI) to sustain its economic growth. In 2020, the country faced a severe economic downturn caused by two major shocks, the social protests in late 2019 and the COVID-19 epidemic. A solid institutional and macroeconomic framework helped Chile recover quickly from these shocks. However, the COVID-19 pandemic exacerbated the already high income inequality, increasing the number of households in a state of economic vulnerability and the number of indebted firms (OECD, 2021[1]).

Figure 1.1. In recent decades, economic growth has supported rising living standards

Trends in GDP and GDP per capita

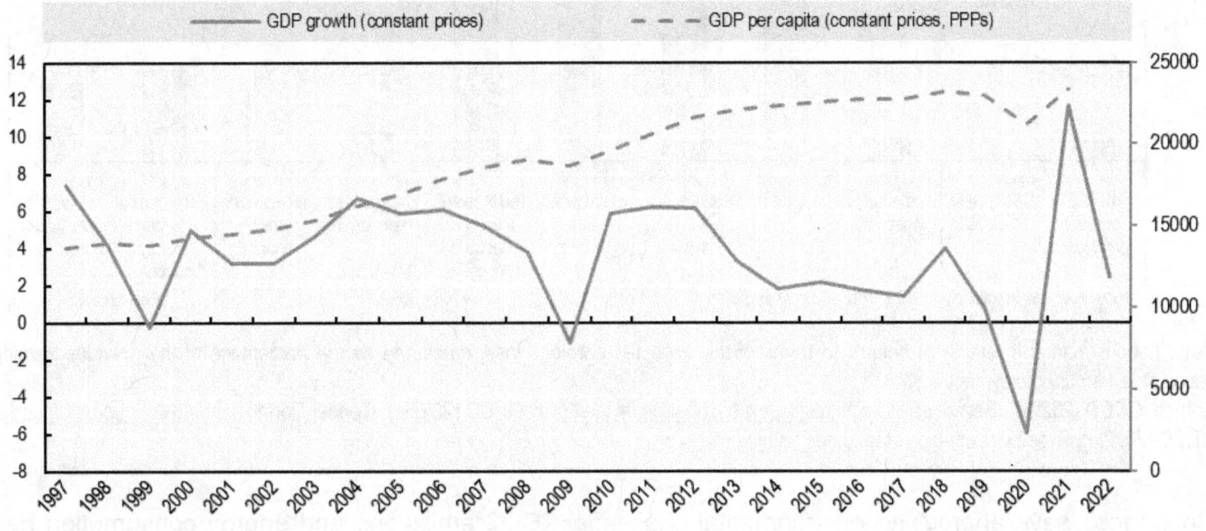

Source: OECD (2022[2]), Annual National Accounts, https://stats.oecd.org/.

Chile has productivity levels below the OECD average (Figure 1.2). Productivity growth has been modest in recent years, due to a combination of factors. The low productivity is partly due to insufficient investment in innovation and R&D, but also to a polarisation of enterprises, i.e. a small number of large, highly productive enterprises and a wide range of small and medium-sized enterprises with low productivity (OECD, 2021[1]). The low economic diversification of the Chilean economy also plays an important role. A significant share of economic activity is concentrated in services, low value-added industries and natural resources. FDI and exports are also largely concentrated in these sectors. Moreover, Chile's dependence on exports of natural resources has increased its vulnerability to external shocks and fluctuations in commodity prices.

Chile's opportunity to diversify its economy and move towards more knowledge-intensive and sustainable activities is hampered by low skill levels. In recent decades, Chile has made remarkable progress in improving the quality of education, but significant challenges remain. The percentage of Chilean adults with at least an upper secondary degree is below the OECD average. While Chile has the best performance for 15-year-olds in reading, science and mathematics among the LAC countries participating in PISA, it ranks among the lowest in the OECD. Gender imbalances persist in education and employment, creating inefficiencies and perpetuating social inequalities. The gender gap among graduates in science, technology, engineering and mathematics (so-called STEM subjects) is higher than the OECD average (OECD, 2021[3]). As globally, women in Chile are more likely to work part-time and informally. They are paid less, although the gender pay gap has decreased recently and is now lower than the OECD average. As elsewhere, a lower percentage of women reach leadership positions, as shown by the share of female managers (Figure 1.2). This share is below the OECD average.

Figure 1.2. Chile underperforms the OECD average across many sustainability indicators

Dashboard of sustainability indicators, 2020

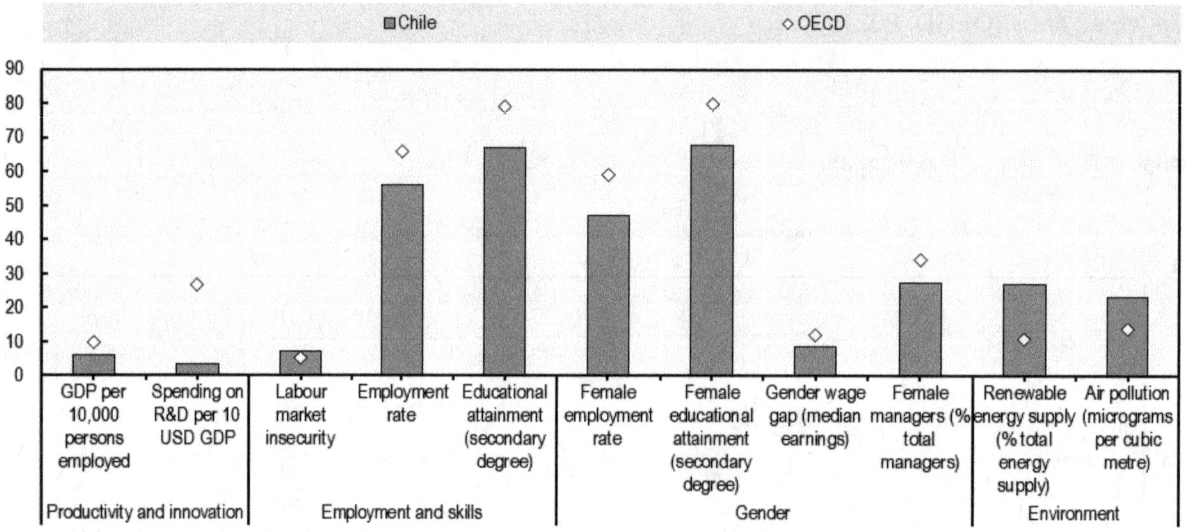

Note: Labour market insecurity is defined in terms of the expected earnings loss, measured as the percentage of the previous earnings, associated with unemployment.
Source: OECD (2022[4]), Better Life Index, https://www.oecdbetterlifeindex.org/; OECD (2022[5]), Gender Portal, https://www.oecd.org/gender/ ; OECD (2022[6]), Green Growth Indicators, https://stats.oecd.org/.

Chile faces several pressing environmental challenges. CO2 emissions and energy consumption have increased in line with the strong economic growth of recent decades. The country still depends on fossil fuels to meet its energy needs. Less than one-third of the total energy supply in Chile comes from renewable sources, although this share is higher than the OECD average (IEA, 2022[7]). Mining for fossil fuels and minerals, deforestation, fishing, and water and land use can deplete natural resources and increase the risk of environmental degradation. Chile has recently made a number of environmental commitments, including achieving carbon neutrality of its economy by 2050, which, if implemented, could reverse these trends.

1.1.2. Diversifying the economy into knowledge-intensive and green activities can help Chile become a more inclusive and sustainable economy

Improving the sophistication of the economy, understood as a wealth of competitive and international firms in a variety of productive sectors, has long been an important policy objective for Chile. Since the 1970s, successive governments have sought to diversify Chile's production base and export basket, including through initiatives to strengthen the role of the private sector. Although these efforts have led to some diversification, economic activity, as well as exports and FDI, remain concentrated in a few low-value added sectors and in natural resources. Dependence on exports of raw materials, particularly copper, and the lack of a strong policy framework for innovation and R&D, human capital development and some regulatory barriers have hindered further economic diversification towards more knowledge-intensive activities.

Economic activity in Chile is focused in sectors that generate less added value per employee, namely services (particularly professional activities, trade and the public sector) and medium and low-tech industries (food, plastics and rubber, and electronics). An important driver of economic activity is also the natural resources sector, including mining and energy, as well as forestry, fishing and agriculture. Chile's strong economic growth in recent decades, also based on the exploitation of natural resources, has not been without costs to the environment, especially in terms of air pollution, water scarcity and pollution, overfishing and deforestation.

Chile is well integrated in global value chains (GVCs), although its position is rather upstream: it mainly exports raw materials and intermediate goods that are then further processed and exported by third countries. Chile's upstream position in GVCs is consistent with its comparative advantage in natural resource sectors, particularly agriculture, fishery, mining and energy, and in medium and low-tech industries, such as chemicals, processed metals, non-metallic minerals, food and beverages. The country also has a competitive edge in exports of transport services, travel and insurance. These sectors have contributed significantly to Chile's economic growth and job creation, but they offer less prospects in terms of sustainable development.

The potential for diversification lies in manufacturing and services activities, which can support innovation, productivity growth, the creation of better jobs and the green transition. Traditional comparative advantages could be leveraged to create new competitive advantages in related sectors with better prospects for sustainable growth. Chile's vast endowment of natural resources and geographical characteristics (the wide variety of climates, including glaciers, volcanoes, rainforests and deserts) make it one of the countries with the highest potential for developing renewable energies (solar, hydroelectric and wind power). The development of these activities, which can help Chile become a more inclusive and green economy, will require new investments in the future, both domestic and foreign.

1.2. FDI can help Chile become a more inclusive and sustainable economy

1.2.1. FDI contributes significantly to sustainable development in Chile

The importance of FDI for the Chilean economy has grown significantly in recent decades, reaching almost the same size as the national GDP in 2020 (a description of the data used in the report can be found in Box 1.1). Since 2012, however, inward FDI flows have decreased, in line with the global trend, but also due to the collapse in commodity prices and recently, the economic recession following the COVID-19 crisis. Through the activities of foreign companies, FDI has contributed significantly to sustainable development in Chile in recent decades. Foreign companies have helped Chile integrate in GVCs and are responsible for a significant share of exports in most sectors, including high-tech and knowledge-intensive sectors. For example, they account for around 80% of exports in telecommunications and information services activities, 55% in IT activities, 50% in electronics and machinery and equipment. Moreover, foreign companies are more export-oriented than Chilean companies: on average, a foreign company exports 32% more of its sales than a domestic company (Figure 1.3).

Foreign firms also participate intensively in domestic value chains, developing business linkages with Chilean companies. They purchase about 73% of their intermediate goods on the domestic market, mainly from small and medium-sized Chilean companies. In addition, they sell about 70% of their production in Chile, partly as inputs to Chilean firms and partly on the final goods market. Several studies point to a positive impact of FDI on productivity and innovation in Chile (Table 2.1). Foreign companies are on average 80% more productive and engage more in R&D activities than Chilean firms.

Figure 1.3. Foreign companies contribute positively to many dimensions of sustainable development

Percentage impact of foreign ownership on firm performance

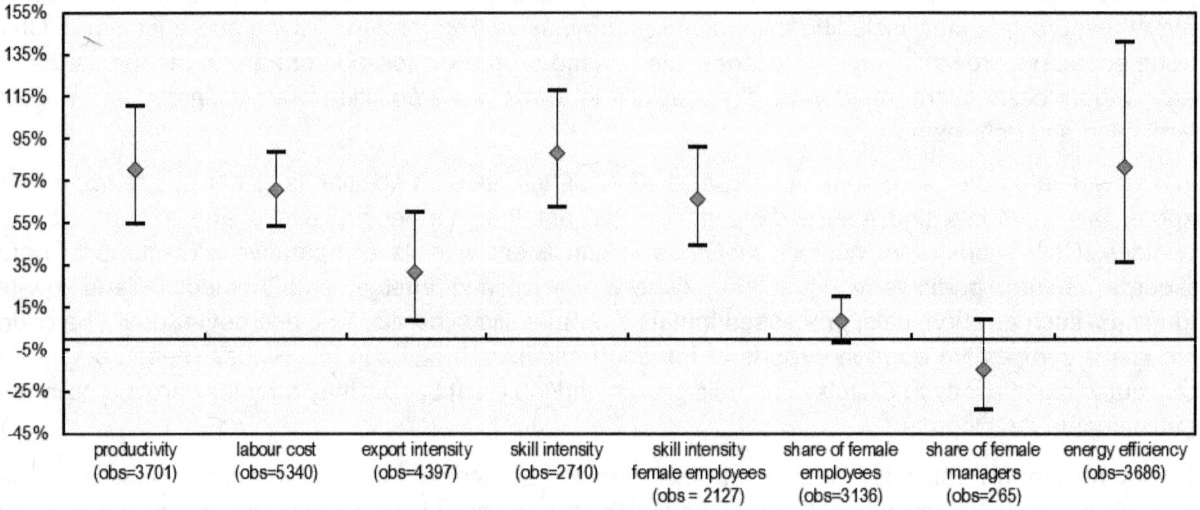

Note: The figure shows the percentage impact of foreign ownership on various business performance variables and their respective confidence interval. When the confidence interval includes 0, the impact is not statistically significant. The percentage impact is calculated using regression analysis. Methodological details can be found in Annex 2.B.
Source: OECD elaboration based on Sexta Encuesta Longitudinal de Empresas (2019[8]), https://www.ine.cl/estadisticas/economia/ciencia-y-tecnologia/encuesta-longitudinal-de-empresas.

Between 2010 and 2020, greenfield FDI generated more than 100 000 jobs in Chile, mainly in mining, energy and manufacturing. However, 1 million dollars of greenfield FDI invested generates fewer jobs in Chile than in other comparator countries as it is directed to sectors with less potential for job creation (i.e. mining and energy). Nevertheless, foreign companies generate a significant number of jobs in many sectors and these jobs are on average better paid and require higher skill levels than those created by domestic companies. Foreign firms have higher proportions of skilled women in most sectors. They are also playing an important role in helping Chile curb its CO2 emissions by promoting a shift from fossil fuels to renewable energy. Foreign investment, particularly greenfield projects, in renewable energy has grown considerably in the past decade and represents today close to 90% of total foreign investment in the energy sector. Foreign firms are also more energy efficient than domestic firms, as they are able to produce a unit of output using less energy.

Box 1.1. Databases used to assess FDI trends and impacts in Chile

Central Bank of Chile's FDI statistics: provides flows and stocks of inward and outward FDI for Chile, from 2012 to 2021, by economic sector and country of origin. In March 2022, the Central Bank of Chile has introduced some improvements in the methodology and data sources used to compile FDI and more generally BOP and IIP statistics. Additional details can be found in Central Bank of Chile (2021[9])

Financial Times' fDi Markets Greenfield FDI database: is a database of crossborder greenfield investments covering all countries. It provides real-time information on capital investment and job creation by economic activity, source country, and location (region). For this study, crossborder greenfield investment projects directed to Chile from 2003 to 2021 were selected, from all countries of origin and covering all economic activities. Economic activities were reclassified to correspond to the ISIC Rev4 sectoral classification.

Thomson Reuters' Mergers and Acquisitions (M&As) database: provides coverage of global M&A deals by country of acquiring company, country of the acquired company and economic activity. For this project, cross-border M&A deals targeting Chilean companies from 2005 to 2021 were selected. Information on the location (headquarters) of the company was retrieved from the business description of the acquired company.

Sexta and Quinta Encuesta Longitudinal de Empresa (ELE6 and ELE5): consist of two representative samples of companies from all economic sectors in Chile in 2019 and 2016/2017, respectively. ELE6 covers 4 006 firms, 391 of which are foreign-owned (a foreign investor directly owns 10% or more of the ordinary shares). ELE5 covers 6 480 companies, 549 of which are foreign-owned. ELE6 and ELE5 provide firm-level information, including on value added, wages, input costs, and employment by gender and skill intensity. ELE5 also includes information on innovation and R&D.

Chile's Internal Revenue Service: information from taxpayer records was used to extract statistical moments for groups of companies based on some relevant characteristics (ownership, company size, location, sector). The extracted information excludes 'non-firm' taxpayers (i.e. households, NGOs or public enterprises) and only considers firms with a median sales greater or equal to USD 100 000 and a median number of workers greater or equal to five.[1]

In addition, several other OECD and non-OECD databases have been used in this report including the OECD FDI statistics, OECD Annual National Accounts, OECD Trade in Value Added (TiVA) indicators, OECD AMNE analytical database, OECD Research & Development Statistics, OECD Gender Portal, OECD Green Growth Indicators, UN Comtrade Database, and the IEA's World Energy Balances.

1.2.2. FDI can play a key role in helping Chile diversify its economy

FDI can help Chile diversify its economy towards more sustainable activities, making it more competitive and resilient to external shocks. In Chile, FDI has traditionally been attracted by natural resources and concentrated in a small number of sectors: mining, energy, finance, trade and low value added sectors (food, chemicals). In the last decade, a smaller share of FDI has been directed to mining, while an increasing share has gone to finance, trade and renewable energy. In general, FDI appears to favour sectors where it can rely on an existing network of local suppliers and a workforce with the required skills. Attracting FDI in a broader spectrum of sectors can contribute to increasing the economic sophistication of the Chilean economy. Foreign firms in Chile are on average more productive, as they use more advanced technologies and are on average more skill-intensive than domestic firms. Foreign firms are also more active in terms of R&D, which is an important driver of innovation and productivity growth. They can contribute indirectly to national productivity, for example by transferring technology and knowledge that can help Chilean companies become more productive.

FDI can also help develop new comparative advantages. Chile specialises and has a comparative advantage in natural resources, medium and low-tech manufacturing industries and some services (transport, tourism, insurance activities, and other business services). FDI can bring new technologies and knowledge to the host economy, which can be used to create new sources of excellence. Foreign companies already present in Chile can be incentivised to invest in new sectors in areas considered strategic from a sustainable development point of view, for example in high-tech, knowledge-intensive and green activities that can boost domestic productivity and improve sustainability. Foreign companies contribute significantly to exports in various technology- and knowledge-intensive sectors, indicating that there is potential to further exploit the benefits of FDI in these sectors. Moreover, diversifying FDI into high-tech and knowledge-intensive activities can lead to the creation of better quality jobs. This is because jobs created in these sectors are on average more skilled and better paid than those created in medium and low-tech industries, mining and construction.

1.3. The policy framework for investment promotion

FDI provides technological and financial resources necessary to improve living standards, boost employment, trigger innovation and deliver green growth. However, FDI does not always go where it is most needed and its impacts on sustainable development are not always positive. The quality of the regulatory environment can determine whether a country can attract sustainable investment, and whether spillovers on the domestic economy can occur. A number of more targeted policies at the intersection of investment policy and sustainable development can also avoid negative implications that may result from the presence of foreign firms, such as crowding out of local SMEs, skills and jobs. These laws, regulations and policy initiatives cannot be considered in silos but in the framework of an adequate and coherent policy mix.

1.3.1. Regulatory restrictions to FDI are limited, but challenges remain for foreign firms

The sound macroeconomic fundamentals, judicial certainty as well as economic and political stability of the past decades have made Chile one of the strongest investment destinations in the LAC region. Chile's statutory restrictions to foreign investment are slightly below the OECD average according to the OECD FDI Regulatory Restrictiveness (FDIRR) index (Figure 1.4). Investment-related policies are non-discriminatory and foreign-owned companies are provided with national treatment, i.e. they receive a treatment no less favourable than domestic companies. Certain market access restrictions are found only in the fisheries and transport sectors, while specific authorisation is required to invest in the exploration and exploitation of hydrocarbons, mining and the production of nuclear energy.

Figure 1.4. Chile's statutory restrictions to FDI are close to the OECD average

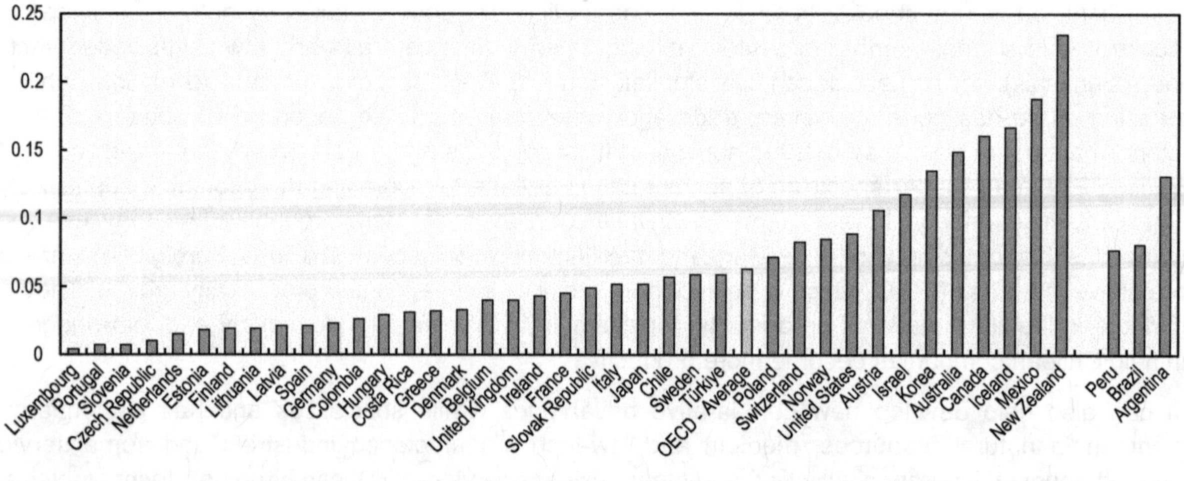

Note: The OECD FDI Regulatory Restrictiveness Index only covers statutory measures discriminating against foreign investors.
Source: OECD (2020[10]), FDI Regulatory Restrictiveness Index, www.oecd.org/investment/fdiindex.htm.

Chile has a competition-friendly regulatory environment that incentivises existing firms to innovate while also supporting the reallocation of resources towards more productive firms. However, one area with significantly more obstacles is the complexity of regulatory procedures, in particular for large investment projects in strategic sectors. The Government of Chile has recently established a digital platform as a single point of contact to deal with sectoral licensing applications; however, significant delays and discretionary decisions are still observed regarding the authorisation of certain investment projects due to the lack of clearly defined approval processes (OECD, 2022[11]). Further digitalisation of business registration and investment licensing processes could help reduce the administrative burden on investors and foster greater certainty and predictability. Similarly, in the case of non-risk economic activities, sectoral licensing requirements could be replaced by a simple prior notification to the authorities. To address these challenges, the government's Productivity Agenda, adopted in 2023, includes more than 40 measures that aim to lift regulatory barriers to productivity growth, including through the structural reform of sectoral permits for investments.

The framework that regulates the public procurement of goods, services and public works is another area that could be further aligned with OECD best practices. While barriers to FDI are low, foreign suppliers of goods and services face higher barriers to participating in public procurement processes than in many OECD countries (OECD, 2021[12]). The buying power of governments can be a lever for promoting sustainable investment practices, in particular in sectors of strategic importance for the Chilean economy. Removing barriers to foreign supplier participation should be combined with the integration of environmental and social criteria in public procurement tenders as well as clearly defined rules to avoid discretionary decisions and ensure integrity and accountability.

1.3.2. Sustainability considerations could be further mainstreamed into Chile's international investment agreements

International investment and trade agreements that are aligned with climate objectives, international labour standards and principles on gender equality and encourage co-operation and monitoring of commitments can complement government efforts to enhance the positive impact of investment on sustainable development (OECD, 2022[12]). Chile is one of the leading Latin American countries in investment treaty-making. The Ministry of Foreign Affairs' Undersecretariat for International Economic Relations (SUBREI) is responsible for negotiating international treaties on economic, trade and investment policy matters. In previous decades, Chile engaged in the negotiation of a wide-ranging network of bilateral investment treaties (BITs) and free trade agreements (FTAs) that led to low tariffs and higher trade and investment, GDP per capital and employment.

In contrast to older agreements, FTAs with investment chapters concluded over the past few years (e.g. FTAs with Canada and the Pacific Alliance countries) have been significantly geared towards sustainable development principles (e.g. gender, labour standards, OECD MNE Guidelines). The inclusion of such provisions is a step in the right direction. However, the bulk of Chile's international investment agreements (IIAs), most of which were concluded in previous decades, does not contain strong commitments to sustainable development principles, and when they do, references are mainly found in the preamble of FTAs (WTI, 2022[13]). Chile could continue efforts to integrate sustainability considerations into new IIAs while at the same time engage in dialogue with its international partners to explore opportunities to update "old generation" agreements (as was the case recently with Canada). Efforts should be also made to improve the quality of these provisions by ensuring that they make reference to a wider set of sustainability principles and international standards (e.g. ILO and RBC standards), and are not limited to the preamble of IIAs.

1.3.3. InvestChile could further improve its capacity to track and measure the contribution of investment promotion activities to the SDGs

Chile's investment promotion agency (IPA), InvestChile, plays a key role in promoting the country as an attractive investment destination and generating leads and investment projects that contribute to sustainable development. In recent years, InvestChile has developed new initiatives to improve the quality of its investment promotion activities and pro-actively target foreign MNEs that contribute to FDI diversification. The prioritisation of low-carbon, technology-intensive and high value added FDI is reflected in InvestChile's portfolio of clients. In 2021, 42% of the supported FDI projects took place in knowledge-intensive services and the technology industry, followed by the agri-food (18%) and energy (11%) sectors (InvestChile, 2022[14]). In terms of value, almost half of supported investments went into the renewables energy sector followed by tourism and mining. InvestChile could consider ways to strengthen its investment promotion activities in key markets abroad to promote Chile as an attractive investment destination, including by establishing a small number of overseas offices in the form of "regional hubs" and by strengthening co-ordination mechanisms with ProChile's international network of offices and the Ministry of Foreign Affairs. Furthermore, the Government of Chile could consider how investment promotion activities and incentive schemes could be better integrated and streamlined to create a systemic support to foreign firms. Effective targeting of quality FDI requires a mix of different types of policy instruments that support firms at every stage of the investment process.

InvestChile is using a basic set of Key Performance Indicators (KPIs) mostly related to the total amount of investment and number of jobs created. These types of indicators are common among OECD IPAs and also reflect the relatively young age of the agency. However, over time OECD IPAs have added additional and more targeted criteria, including those related to sustainability and inclusiveness (Sztajerowska and Volpe Martincus, 2021[15]). In addition, numerous OECD IPAs developed dedicated sustainability scoring mechanisms to guide their prioritisation efforts. In this context, building on examples from other OECD countries, it could be considered how tracking and measuring InvestChile's contribution to the SDGs, and sustainable and inclusive development more generally, could be improved further. The OECD stands ready to assist the agency in this process.

The recent adoption of a new National Strategy for the Promotion of Foreign Investment provides a good opportunity to clarify the role of government institutions that should be involved in the implementation of policies at the intersection of investment promotion and sustainable development. The strategy presents a new investment prioritisation framework that relies on criteria linking investment projects to specific sustainable development outcomes. The latter will be also linked to concrete policy initiatives and government reforms that will seek to address regulatory barriers to FDI and strengthen the capacities of the Chilean economy. The successful implementation of the strategy will require increased attention on the issues of policy alignment and co-ordination as well as the use of robust monitoring and evaluation tools to identify policy inefficiencies and assess the impact of investment promotion policies on the Chilean economy. InvestChile's co-ordinating role should be strengthened through the agency's participation in high-level government councils that deal with sustainable development policy areas such as the Inter-Ministerial Committee for Science, Technology, Knowledge and Innovation, the Inter-Ministerial Committee for Sustainable Productive Development, and the Council of Ministers for Sustainability and Climate Change.

1.4. Policies at the intersection of investment promotion and sustainable development

1.4.1. Public support to R&D-intensive investment could be better co-ordinated and targeted

Chile provides one of the lowest levels of total government support for business R&D among OECD and partner economies (OECD, 2021[16]). The Chilean support to business R&D – both direct (e.g. grants, loans) and indirect (e.g. tax relief) – ranks far from top innovators such as the US, Canada, France and Portugal. A tax incentive for extramural R&D was first introduced in 2008, whereby enterprises operating in Chile are entitled to a 35% tax credit for R&D certified contracts entered into with a registered research centre. The low level of R&D government support could be a barrier to attracting additional investment in knowledge-intensive activities, in particular given that certain LAC countries may provide more generous schemes (e.g. Brazil, Colombia). The low uptake of R&D tax relief by Chilean SMEs may also be a sign of weak domestic capacities in the area of innovation, which could be an important barrier for domestic enterprises to develop value chain linkages and knowledge-intensive partnerships with foreign MNEs operating in Chile. The government could consider further adjusting the current scheme to make it more attractive and less burdensome for both foreign and domestic firms who seek to engage in innovative activities. Such a reform should be also accompanied by measures to remedy a lack of awareness of the tax credit among smaller enterprises and other R&D institutions that operate in FDI-intensive sectors.

Direct government funding in the form of grants and loans could be also increased and better co-ordinated and targeted in order to promote Chile's strategic priorities in the area of sustainable development and FDI diversification. Financial support for innovative and productive investments is offered by a number of public institutions. For instance, the Chilean Economic Development Agency (CORFO) has launched several financing calls inviting domestic and foreign firms to benefit from preferential pricing schemes and other financial support for investments in the mineral resources, agricultural and green hydrogen industries. Similarly, the National Agency for Research and Development (ANID), which reports to the Ministry of Science, Technology, Knowledge and Innovation, offers a wide range of short-term funding tenders as well as technical assistance programmes. However, existing institutional arrangements, funding mechanisms and policy mix lack an overarching framework that could identify strategic opportunities across sectors and provide the necessary long-term finance to diversify the country's production structure and hasten its transition towards a knowledge-based economy.

The Government of Chile is currently considering ways to streamline and consolidate its financial incentives framework. One option would be to leverage the potential of the new Inter-Ministerial Committee for Sustainable Productive Development to co-ordinate the administration and granting of the various incentive schemes in a more coherent way. Another option would be for the government to leverage the already established Banco del Estado and/or CORFO to make available a diverse portfolio of funding tools (e.g. loans, grants, guarantees, equity investments) and network-building initiatives to crowd-in private investors, including foreign MNEs, through risk-sharing, co-financing strategies and public-private partnerships. It will be important that the bank relies on clear strategies, policies and targets that align its activities and financing tools with Chile's investment promotion, innovation and low-carbon priorities. Such alignment can be achieved through the participation of key government agencies such as InvestChile, CORFO and ProChile in the management of the new incentives framework. The activities should be also evaluated periodically to ensure that the benefits outweigh potential costs (e.g. economic distortions, forgone public revenue, etc).

1.4.2. Investment promotion has a crucial role to play in supporting skills development

Existing skills imbalances in the Chilean labour market can be a significant barrier for foreign MNEs that seek to invest in knowledge-intensive activities. Chile ranks in the bottom 20% of OECD countries for the skills development of youth and adults while around half of Chilean workers has only basic proficiency in problem solving skills in technology-rich environments (OECD, 2019[17]). Qualification mismatch is very close to the OECD average; however, Chile has one of the highest prevalence of skills mismatch in OECD countries and a larger-than-average proportion of adults with low literacy and numeracy skills.

Regarding its labour market regime, Chile has one of the highest shares of temporary employment in the OECD area and a high job turnover, which negatively affect domestic and foreign firms' incentives to invest in job training. The government has sought to encourage on-the-job training through a tax franchise scheme, which allows companies to benefit from tax credits if their workers participate in training courses offered by the National Training and Employment Service (SENCE). However, the number of workers benefitting from the scheme has been following a downward trend over the past decade, and there is little involvement of employers on the type of training that their workers get. Foreign MNEs operating in Chile should be further incentivised to undertake training activities for their own employees and for their local suppliers. Existing training incentives should become flexible enough to allow foreign MNEs to tailor their content and scope to the needs of their employees.

Although skills development programmes are implemented by various sectoral ministries and their implementing agencies, evidence suggests that they are not always of good quality, face challenges in targeting their objective population and are insufficiently aligned with the needs of the labour market (Bogliaccini et al., 2022[18]). There is also a lack in demand for training and, when it occurs, training benefits mostly highly educated workers (e.g. senior professionals) or workers in occupations with high demand for specific skills. Skills development programmes should better target job seekers and vulnerable groups of workers, including women and unemployed, who may be adversely affected by foreign MNEs' changing needs or FDI's diversification away from natural resources sectors. To this end, sectoral retraining programmes can be more impactful than general training courses, as they reduce skills shortages in target sectors where FDI may crowd out competitors unable to retain their talented staff. InvestChile should co-ordinate with SENCE, CORFO and Chile's labour intermediation offices for the development of joint programmes and initiatives that allow foreign MNEs to find the skills they need. The agency could also further promote sectors and activities in alignment with the existing skills base and provide appropriate information to investors on labour market characteristics.

If Chile wants to diversify into high-tech and knowledge-intensive activities, including by attracting more FDI in these sectors, it needs to invest in a broader set of skills, beyond those required in sectors where FDI is already present. This will require robust skills anticipation systems that involve the investment community and allow to design evidence-based and forward-looking programmes that match expected skills needs in various industrial sectors. The Advisory Council on Technical and Vocational Training could play a more active role in the implementation of skills needs assessments and, in collaboration with InvestChile, help better identify the skills needs driven by FDI.

1.4.3. Promoting green FDI will require reforms in carbon pricing and incentives for renewable energy expansion

Creating an enabling environment for green and low-carbon investment has been an important and longstanding policy priority for the Government of. Recent initiatives have focused on setting low-carbon transition targets and long-term policy strategies that send investors, including foreign ones, strong signals regarding the government's climate ambitions. Chile is the first Latin American country that made emission targets legally binding through its 2022 Framework Law on Climate Change. It has also been a regional leader in attracting FDI in renewable energy by addressing regulatory barriers in the energy market and facilitating the connection of the electrical system to renewable energy plants. Despite progress, Chile still heavily relies on carbon energies due to the weight of the transport sector and the growth in the energy-intensive needs of certain industries (e.g. mining).

Chile's long-term goal of 100% zero-emission electricity generation and 80% renewable energy by 2050 will require to keep a fast pace of investment in clean energy. Achieving this target will require strong co-ordination for the implementation of targeted policies, in particular for hard-to-abate sectors and industries for which FDI could significantly contribute to their decarbonisation. The current carbon pricing framework should be reviewed with the aim to increase carbon taxes at levels comparable to international standards and improve their sectoral coverage. In terms of regulation, regulatory restrictions in the transport sector, a major CO2 pollutant, should be lifted to attract FDI that contributes to the transfer of know-how and the deployment of low-carbon technologies.

Additional measures could be also explored for the attraction of private investment in Chile's emerging green hydrogen industry. Given the early technological maturity of hydrogen technologies and the high risks involved, regulatory reforms across the value chain and targeted public policy interventions will be necessary to create the conditions for private investment. For the initial phase, time-limited financial support schemes could reduce the investment risk for industry and close part of the cost differential with other types of energy sources (IEA, 2021[19]). Specific financial tools by the Banco del Estado or CORFO, as suggested previously, could help in the deployment of grants, concessional loans and guarantees to make investment projects more bankable. Scaling up low-carbon hydrogen and use will also require timely investments in enabling infrastructure, including new transmission lines (for low-carbon electricity to reach the electrolysers for on-grid projects), hydrogen transport and storage infrastructure and port terminals. Demand-side bottlenecks could be also resolved for investments to scale up. However, if the Government of Chile decides to pursue the development of the green hydrogen industry, uncertainties about the demand for green hydrogen versus other energy-related sources and technologies, which are currently more cost-competitive, should be taken into consideration since they are a key obstacle for mobilising private capital.

References

Bogliaccini, J. et al. (2022), *(Un)Employment and skills formation in Chile: An exploration of the effects of training in labour market transitions*. [19]

Central Bank of Chile (2021), *Balanza de Pagos de Chile, Positión de Inversión International y Deuda Externa*, https://si3.bcentral.cl/estadisticas/Principal1/Informes/AnuarioBDP/pdf/ANUARIO_BP_2021.pdf. [9]

Government of Chile, The National Institute of Statistics and the Ministry of the Economy (2019), *Encuesta Longitudinal de Empresas 6 (ELE6)*, https://www.ine.cl/estadisticas/economia/ciencia-y-tecnologia/encuesta-longitudinal-de-empresas. [8]

IEA (2022), *World Energy Balances*, https://www.iea.org/data-and-statistics/data-product/world-energy-balances. [7]

IEA (2021), *Hydrogen in Latin America: From near-term opportunities to large-scale deployment*, OECD Publishing, Paris, https://doi.org/10.1787/68467068-en. [20]

InvestChile (2022), *Foreign Investment in Chile in 2021*, https://investchile.gob.cl/wp-content/uploads/2022/03/reporte-ied-en-chile-a-marzo2022.pdf. [15]

OECD (2022), *Annual National Accounts*, https://stats.oecd.org/. [2]

OECD (2022), *Better Life Index*, https://www.oecdbetterlifeindex.org/. [4]

OECD (2022), *FDI Qualities Policy Toolkit*, OECD Publishing, Paris, https://doi.org/10.1787/7ba74100-en. [13]

OECD (2022), *Gender Portal*, https://www.oecd.org/gender/. [5]

OECD (2022), *Green Growth Indicators*, https://stats.oecd.org/. [6]

OECD (2022), *OECD Economic Surveys: Chile 2022*, OECD Publishing, Paris, https://doi.org/10.1787/311ec37e-en. [11]

OECD (2021), *Gender Equality in Chile: Towards a Better Sharing of Paid and Unpaid Work*, https://doi.org/10.1787/6cc8ea3e-en. [3]

OECD (2021), *OECD Economic Surveys: Chile 2021*, https://doi.org/10.1787/79b39420-en. [1]

OECD (2021), *OECD Product Market Regulation Indicators*, http://www.oecd.org/economy/reform/indicators-of-product-market-regulation/. [12]

OECD (2021), *R&D Tax Incentives: Chile, 2021*, http://www.oecd.org/sti/rd-tax-stats-chile.pdf. [17]

OECD (2020), *OECD FDI Regulatory Restrictiveness Index*, http://www.oecd.org/investment/fdiindex.htm. [10]

OECD (2019), *2019 OECD Skills Strategy: Chile*, http://www.oecd.org/chile/Skills-Strategy-Chile-EN.pdf. [18]

Sztajerowska, M. and C. Volpe Martincus (2021), *Together or apart: investment promotion agencies' prioritisation and monitoring and evaluation for sustainable investment promotion*, https://www.oecd.org/daf/inv/investment-policy/Investment-Insights-Investment-Promotion-Prioritisation-OECD.pdf. [16]

WTI (2022), *Sustainable Development in Chilean International Investment Agreements*, World Trade Institute, http://www.wti.org/media/filer_public/d3/96/d3967dfa-0393-42bf-a3e9-cb519943562e/wti_working_paper_07_2022_sustainable_development_in_chilean_international_investment_agreements.pdf. [14]

Notes

[1] The information has been compiled in accordance with legal standards of aggregation that prevent the disclosure of private information. The Internal Revenue Service assumes no responsibility or warranty for the use or application of this information.

2 Trends and impacts of FDI in Chile

This chapter examines FDI trends in Chile in terms of sector, regional distribution, country of origin and mode of entry of the foreign investors (i.e. greenfield FDI, M&As). It also analyses how FDI contributes to important sustainable development priorities in Chile, namely trade and GVC integration; productivity and innovation; job quality and skills, including for women; and the low-carbon transition. It also discusses how FDI can help diversify the Chilean economy towards sectors with better prospects for sustainable development.

2.1. Trends and characteristics of FDI in Chile

2.1.1. The importance of FDI for the Chilean economy has increased over the past decade

A small, open economy rich in natural resources, Chile is a particularly attractive destination for foreign direct investment (FDI). The relevance of FDI for the Chilean economy is shown by the FDI to GDP ratio, which has grown significantly over the last decade, reaching 98% in 2020. Chile has one of the highest FDI to GDP ratios in the OECD area, above those of other Latin American and Caribbean (LAC) countries such as Colombia and Mexico and other OECD countries of similar economic size, such as the Czech Republic, and rich in natural resources, such as Australia. In 2021, the FDI to GDP ratio decreased due to the relatively larger decline in FDI flows compared to GDP during the COVID-19 crisis, similar to what was observed in other countries (Figure 2.1, Panel A).

FDI flows to Chile have been declining since 2012 (Panel B). This negative trend, observed in many other countries, is partly attributable to a slowdown in international production and the retrenchment of global value chains (UNCTAD, 2018[1]). The COVID-19 pandemic and its disruptive effects on the activities of multinational enterprises (MNEs) have further contributed to the decline in FDI flows globally. In Chile, as in the rest of Latin America, the decline was particularly pronounced due to the collapse of commodity prices and the economic recession that followed the COVID-19 crisis (UNCTAD, 2021[2]). Data for 2021 show a slight recovery of FDI flows to Chile, however.

Figure 2.1. The FDI to GDP ratio has increased over the last decade, despite the decline in FDI flows

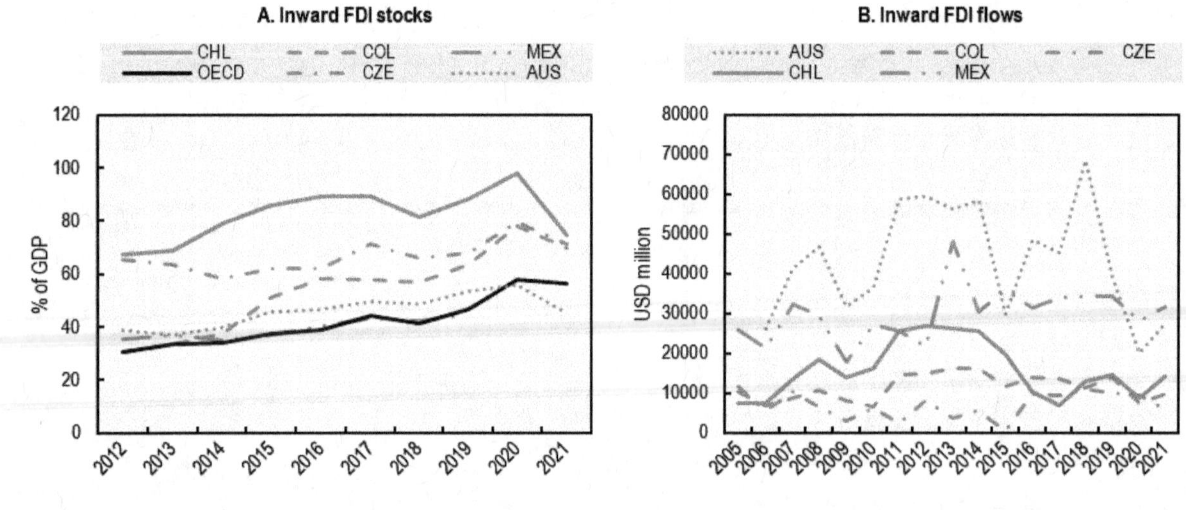

Source: OECD (2022[3]), FDI Statistics, https://stats.oecd.org/.

2.1.2. FDI is largely concentrated in mining, energy and finance

Chile's endowment of natural resources explains the large share of FDI in the mining sector (Figure 2.2). In 2021, 28% of FDI stocks were in the mining sector, particularly metals. While the stocks of FDI in mining has remained more or less unchanged since 2012, the relative share has decreased by 6 percentage points. Meanwhile, FDI in financial services and energy, particularly renewable energy, has gained importance in the Chilean FDI landscape. Over the 2012-21 period, the share of FDI stocks in financial services increased from 6% to 15%, while the share in the energy sector grew from 8% to 15%. It is possible, however, that some of these shares are underestimated as a significant amount of FDI stocks provided by the Central Bank of Chile is 'not allocated' (24% in 2021).

Figure 2.2. Mining, finance and energy receive the bulk of FDI

Inward FDI stocks by sector

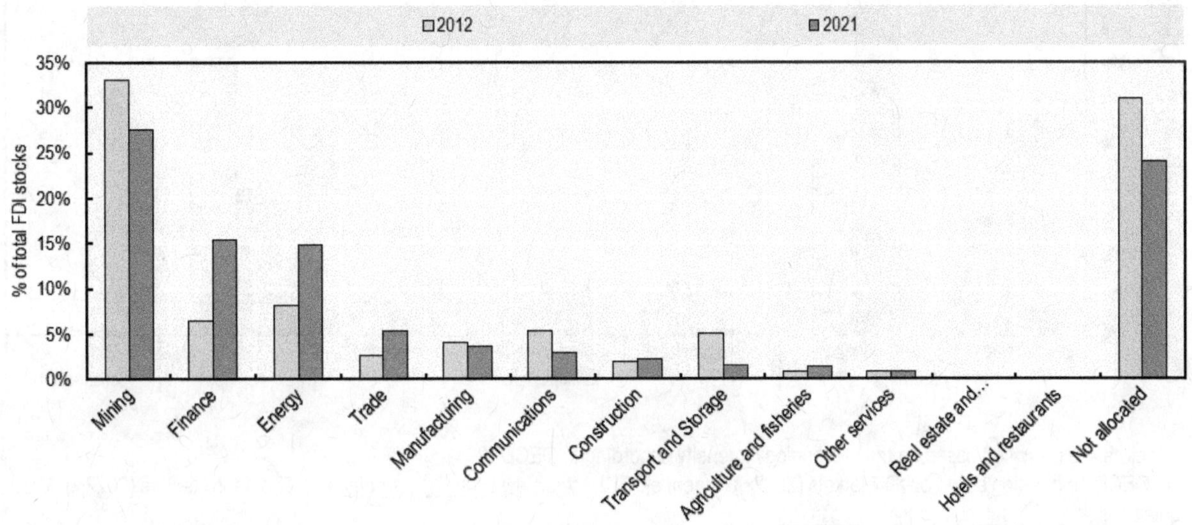

Source: OECD elaboration based on Central Bank of Chile (2022[4]), Foreign Direct Investment, https://www.bcentral.cl/en/home

With respect to the mode of entry of foreign investors, the data show significant differences between greenfield FDI (i.e. the creation of new business enterprises in the host economy and additional injection of funds to existing ones.) and merger and acquisitions (M&As) (Figure 2.3). Greenfield FDI is concentrated in the energy sector (44%), especially renewables, and mining (coal, oil and gas and metals extraction) (27%). Smaller shares go to the services sector (19%) and manufacturing (9%). Within services, most greenfield FDI is directed to communications, business services, transportation, and finance, while the main targets in manufacturing are medium and low-tech industries such as metals, chemicals, and food. A very small share of greenfield FDI (1%) is channelled to construction. M&A deals are concentrated in services (36%), especially finance and transportation, mining (26%) and energy (23%). A smaller share goes to manufacturing (14%), in particular to medium- and low-tech chemical and food products and high-tech pharmaceuticals. A negligible share of M&A transactions are concluded in construction (1%).

Figure 2.3. Greenfield FDI and M&A deals prevail in energy, mining and services

Cross-border greenfield FDI and M&A deals cumulated over 2010-21

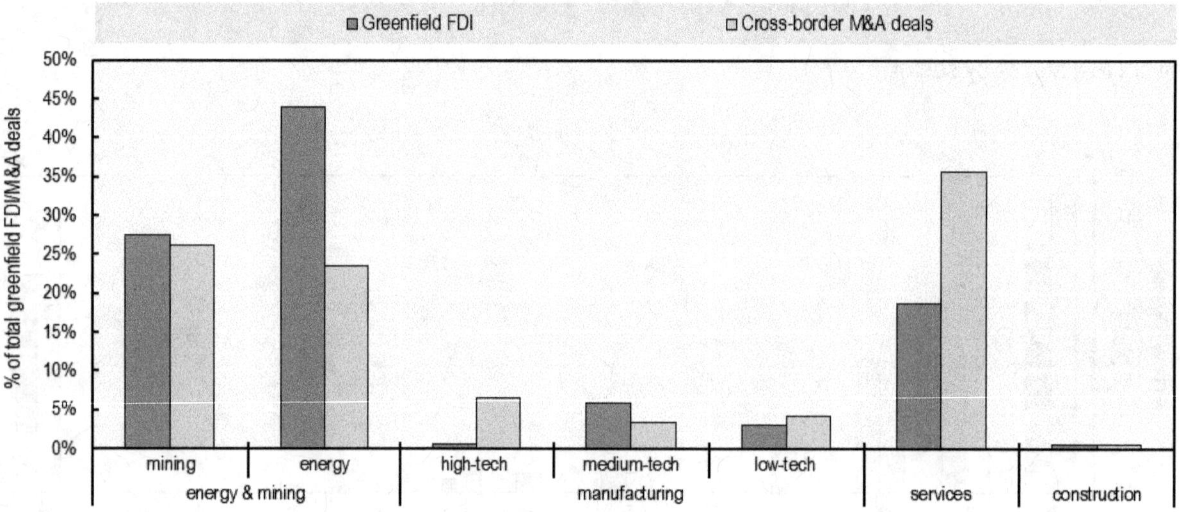

Note: Sectors are classified based on their technology intensity according to OECD (2011[5])
Source: OECD elaboration based on fDi Markets (2022[6]), greenfield FDI, https://www.fdimarkets.com/; and Thomson Reuters (2022[7]), Mergers & Acquisitions, https://legal.thomsonreuters.com/en.

2.1.3. Antofagasta, Atacama and Santiago attract most FDI

Regardless of the mode of entry, FDI appears to be concentrated in a few regions. Between 2010 and 2021, greenfield FDI was mainly directed to three regions: Antofagasta, Atacama and the Metropolitan Region (Santiago) (Figure 2.4). This is not surprising considering that mines are located in Antofagasta and Atacama and that Santiago is the main economic centre of Chile.[1] While in Antofagasta and Atacama greenfield investments were mainly directed at the mining and energy sectors, in the Metropolitan Region they covered a wider range of sectors, such as communications, financial services, restaurants and hotels, transportation services and the food industry. A considerable number of jobs in the Metropolitan Region have also been created in renewable energy.

Most of the cross-border M&A transactions in the period 2010-21 also took place in the Metropolitan Region (Panel B). It is likely, however, that this figure is overestimated because in the data available for this study, the location of M&As is often based on the company's headquarters (HQ), even if the company's facilities are located in other regions. This is the case of several mining companies whose headquarters are located in Santiago, while their mining facilities are located in Antofagasta and Atacama. In addition, information on the location of the acquired or merged company was not provided for about 36% of the M&A transactions that materialise during this period.

Regional disparities in FDI are much higher in Chile than in other OECD countries. Moreover, disparities in FDI remain considerable even when population density is taken into account, i.e. when FDI is considered in per capita terms. A recent OECD study shows that regional disparities in FDI are correlated with labour productivity discrepancies, suggesting that there is a strong link between foreign investment and the level of productivity at the regional level (OECD, Forthcoming[8]).

Figure 2.4. Greenfield FDI and M&A deals are concentrated in a few regions

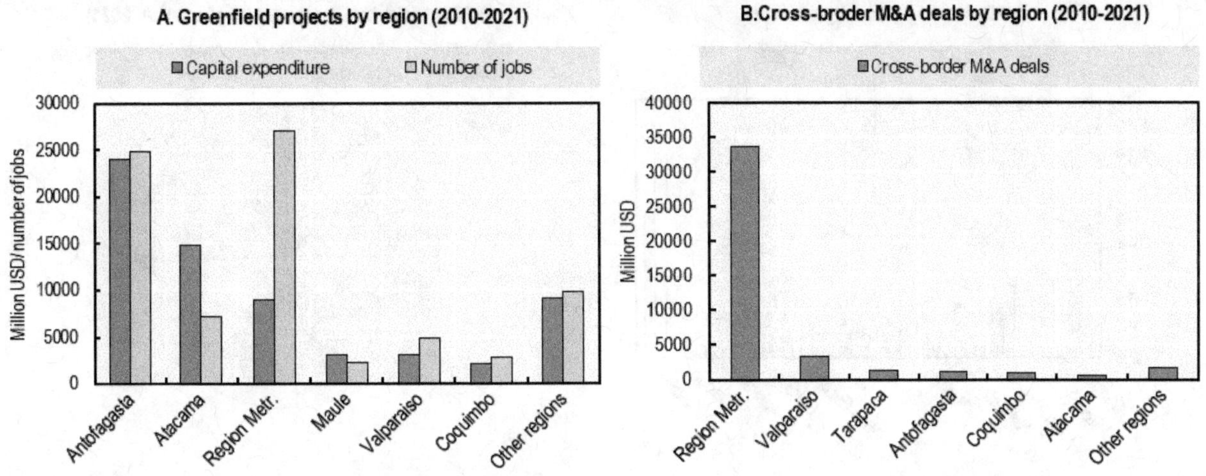

Source: OECD elaboration based on fDi Markets (2022[6]), greenfield FDI, https://www.fdimarkets.com/; and Thomson Reuters (2022[7]), Mergers & Acquisitions, https://legal.thomsonreuters.com/en.

2.1.4. Companies from Europe and Northern America are the leading investors

More than 62% of the FDI stocks are investments from Europe, particularly the Netherlands, the United Kingdom, Spain and Italy, and North America, namely Canada and the United States (Figure 2.5, Panel A). About 13% came from Latin America, a much smaller share considering the geographical proximity. The main investors from Latin America and the Caribbean were Brazil, Colombia, Bermuda and Mexico (Panel B). Moreover, while FDI stocks from Canada, Spain, the United Kingdom and Italy grew between 2012 and 2021 in both absolute and relative terms, those from the United States and Latin America declined. Negative FDI stocks were recorded for Argentina and Peru.[2]

The low importance of South American partners for Chile is a long-term issue. The low economic and trade integration of Latin American countries appear to be explained by high costs of trade within the region, due to poor transport and logistics infrastructure, complicated and non-transparent non-tariff measures (e.g. product standards), regulatory constraints on trade in services, as well as the low degree of participation in GVCs of some partners (e.g. Argentina and Brazil) (Gonzalez, 2017[9]; OECD, 2015[10]).

Figure 2.5. More than 60% of FDI stocks originate from Europe and North America

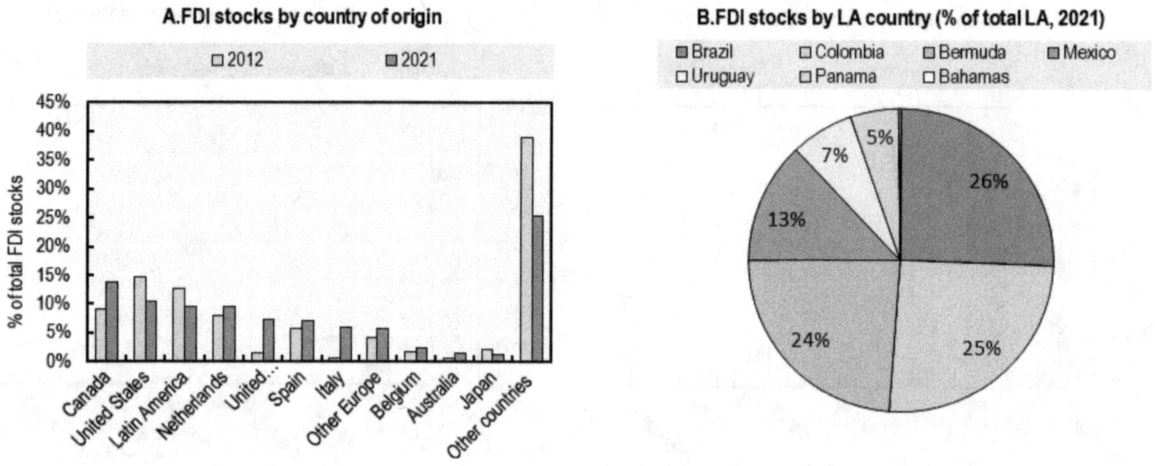

Source: OECD elaboration based on Central Bank of Chile (2022[4]), Foreign Direct Investment, https://www.bcentral.cl/en/home

About 25% of FDI stocks in 2021 provided by the Central Bank of Chile cannot be allocated to a specific country, however. Thus, it is possible that the shares for some countries are underestimated. Moreover, as the FDI data of the Central Bank of Chile follow the principle of the immediate investor (and not that of the ultimate investor), they do not provide an accurate picture of the origin of investments when a parent (ultimate) company invests in Chile through another (immediate) subsidiary in a third country.

Thomson Reuters' M&A deals provide a more accurate picture of the origin of these investments, as they distinguish between ultimate and immediate investor. The data show that most of the cross-border M&A transactions in Chile in the last decade were concluded by European and North American firms, roughly confirming the picture that emerges from the Central Bank of Chile's FDI data (Figure 2.6, Panel A). The data also show that in recent years a significant share of M&A transactions in Chile have been concluded by Chinese companies. Although growing rapidly, FDI from China remains marginal in the Chilean landscape (around 0.2% in 2021 according to the Central Bank of Chile's FDI data). However, it is also possible that some Chinese companies invest via other countries (e.g. the Cayman Islands) and that such flows are not allocated to China (Sutherland, El-Gohari and Matthews, 2010[11]). The sector of the investment varies greatly depending on the country of origin of the companies. US, Canadian, Spanish, British and Qatari companies concluded M&A deals mainly in the service sector, in particular finance, telecommunications and transport (Panel B). The M&A transactions of Chinese, Italian and Argentinean companies mainly concerned the energy sector, while those of Japanese investors the mining sector.

The predominant role of European and North American companies is also confirmed by greenfield FDI data (Figure 2.7, Panel A). The data also show that China's greenfield investment was 10 times higher in 2016-21 than in 2010-15. China's share in total greenfield FDI received by Chile between 2016 and 2021 is still small (about 2%), however. Most of the top investors favoured energy, particularly renewable energy, and mining (Panel B).

Figure 2.6. M&A deals by Chinese companies have grown dramatically over the past five years

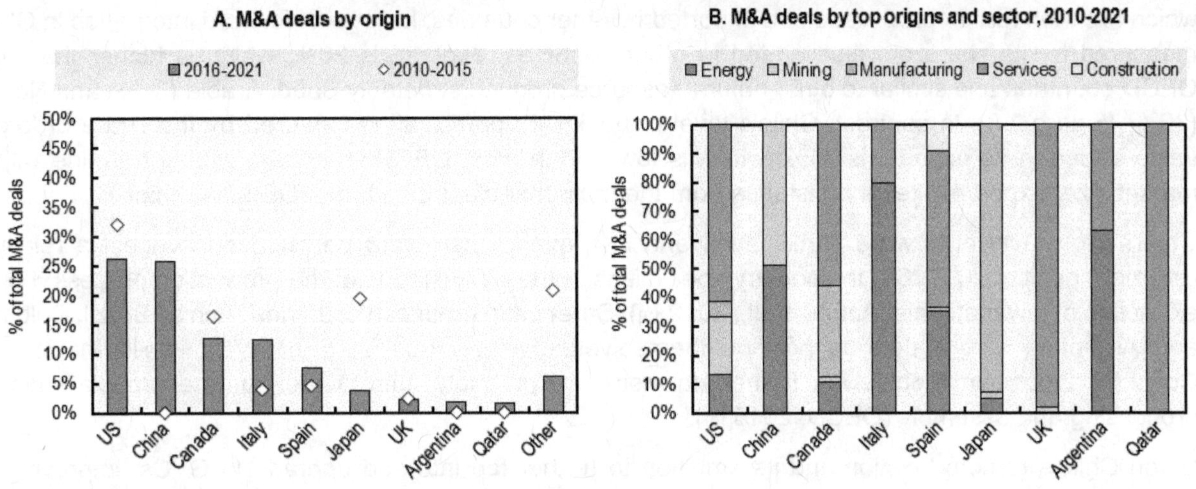

Source: OECD elaboration based on Thomson Reuters (2022[7]), Mergers & Acquisitions, https://legal.thomsonreuters.com/en.

Figure 2.7. Greenfield FDI from the top investors favour energy and mining

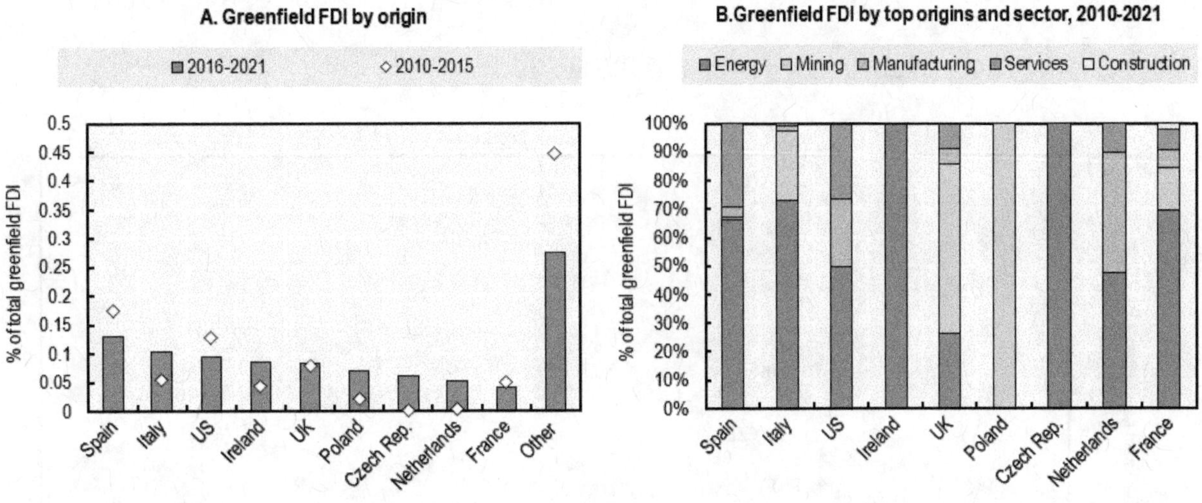

Source: OECD elaboration based on fDi Markets (2022[6]), greenfield FDI, https://www.fdimarkets.com/.

2.2. FDI supports trade and integration in global value chains

2.2.1. Chile participates in GVC mainly through its forward linkages

Participation in GVCs brings new opportunities for productivity growth and innovation. Countries participate in GVCs by using imported inputs in their exports (backward participation in GVCs) or by providing intermediate inputs to third country exports (forward participation). Productivity spillovers can occur from both backward and forward participation in GVCs. Backward participation enables countries to use inputs that are not available in the domestic economy or that have an advantage in terms of price or quality, while upstream participation allows countries to acquire technology and knowledge from export destinations (Criscuolo and Timmis, 2017[12]).

Chile's level of forward integration into GVCs is high, as would be expected from a net exporter of natural resources. Like many natural resource producers, Chile exports mainly primary and intermediate products, which are then further processed and exported by other countries. Its level of forward integration in GVCs, measured by its share of value added in other countries' exports, is 26%, which is higher than most OECD countries and similar to other natural resource producers, notably Saudi Arabia (34%) and Norway (39%) (Figure 2.8). In contrast, Chile's level of backward participation captured by the share of foreign value added in its exports, is 14%, which is lower than most OECD countries, although in line with its market size, export basket and distance from the main manufacturing hubs (OECD, 2015[10]).

Chile's high level of forward participation and low level of backward participation suggest a relatively upstream position in GVCs: the country specialises in the early stages of the production process, i.e. the extraction of raw materials (Antràs et al., 2012[13]). Other Latin American countries such as Brazil, Colombia and Argentina also appear to position themselves relatively upstream in GVCs, while Mexico and Costa Rica position themselves further downstream, probably due to their greater specialisation in processing and assembly (OECD, 2015[10]).

Given Chile's remote location and its ambition to further tap into and upgrade in GVCs, improving the competitiveness of backbone services (e.g. telecommunications, air and rail transport) and logistics will be crucial. OECD estimates show that logistics accounts for about one-fifth of the total value of output in Chile's manufacturing sector, which is over two times higher than the OECD average (OECD, 2015[10]). This suggests that a reduction in logistics costs is estimated to have a greater impact on Chile's total manufacturing output than in most OECD countries. The availability and sustainability of energy, water and transport services are also key considerations for the future growth of the mining sector in Chile.

Figure 2.8. Chile has an upstream position in GVCs

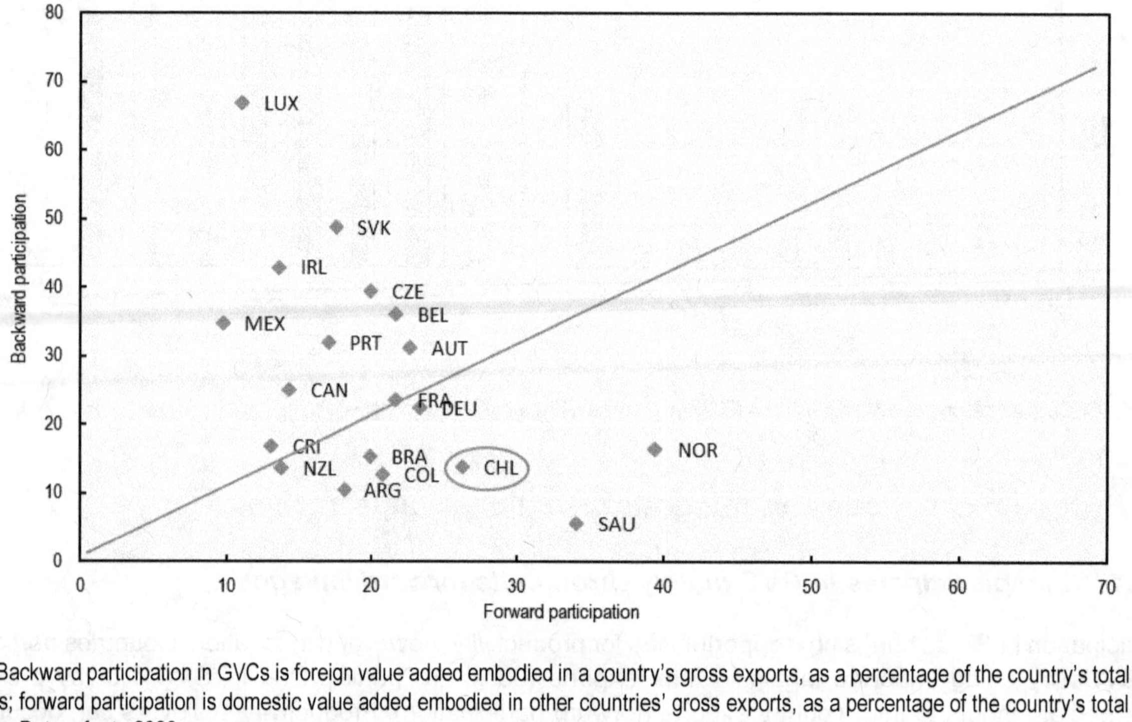

Note: Backward participation in GVCs is foreign value added embodied in a country's gross exports, as a percentage of the country's total gross exports; forward participation is domestic value added embodied in other countries' gross exports, as a percentage of the country's total gross exports. Data refer to 2020

Source: OECD (2021[14]), TiVA indicators, https://www.oecd.org/sti/ind/measuring-trade-in-value-added.htm

2.2.2. Chile has a comparative advantage in natural resources, medium- and low-tech manufacturing and some services

Chile has a comparative advantage in several activities in the natural resources sector and medium- and low-tech manufacturing, i.e. it exports relatively more in these activities than the rest of the world (Box 2.1). In particular, the country has a traditional comparative advantage in the production and exports of metals (copper; iron; silver and platinum; lead), several agriculture and fisheries products (fish; vegetables; fruit; and nuts), chemical products (fertilisers; inorganic chemicals); basic and fabricated-metal products (crude iron, spiegeleisen, sponge iron, iron or steel granules and powders and ferroalloys; metal containers for storage or transport); non-metallic minerals; food and beverages (processed foods, animal oils and beverages); textiles and clothing (wool and other animal hair); and wood and paper (wood, pulp, cork and paper (Figure 2.9).

It also has an emerging comparative advantage in some activities in metals (ferrous waste and scrap; remelting scrap ingots of iron or steel), textiles and clothing (worn clothing and other worn textile articles) and chemicals. In addition, it has a declining comparative advantage in agriculture (unmilled maise and cereals); food and beverages (dairy products; meat products; tobacco); metals (ores and precious metal concentrates); and chemicals (starches, inulin and wheat gluten, albuminoid substances, glues). It has no traditional or emerging comparative advantage in any of the high-tech activities, nor in most of the medium-tech activities. Chile has a strong comparative advantage also in several service sectors, particularly in transport, travel, other business services and insurance services (Figure 2.10). At the same time, it has a higher opportunity cost than its trading partners in computer and information services, personal, cultural and recreational services, and financial services.

Overall, Chile seems to be far from developing comparative advantages in high-tech and knowledge-intensive sectors (e.g. Electronics and optical products, other transport equipment, computer and information services) which offer greater opportunities in terms of sustainable development. These sectors contribute more in terms of added value and innovation and tend to create more skilled and better paid jobs.

Figure 2.9. Chile has a comparative advantage in natural resources and several medium-low-tech industries

Number of sub-sectors by Revealed Comparative Advantage (RCA) category

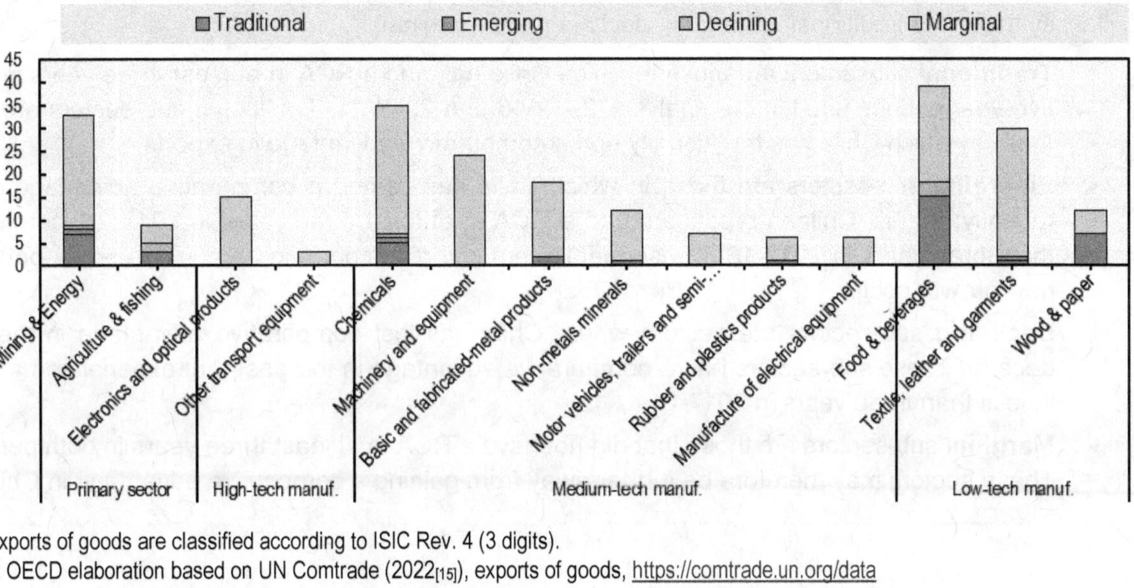

Note: Exports of goods are classified according to ISIC Rev. 4 (3 digits).
Source: OECD elaboration based on UN Comtrade (2022[15]), exports of goods, https://comtrade.un.org/data

Figure 2.10. Chile has a comparative advantage in transportation, insurance services, travel and other business services

RCA >1 indicates a comparative advantage

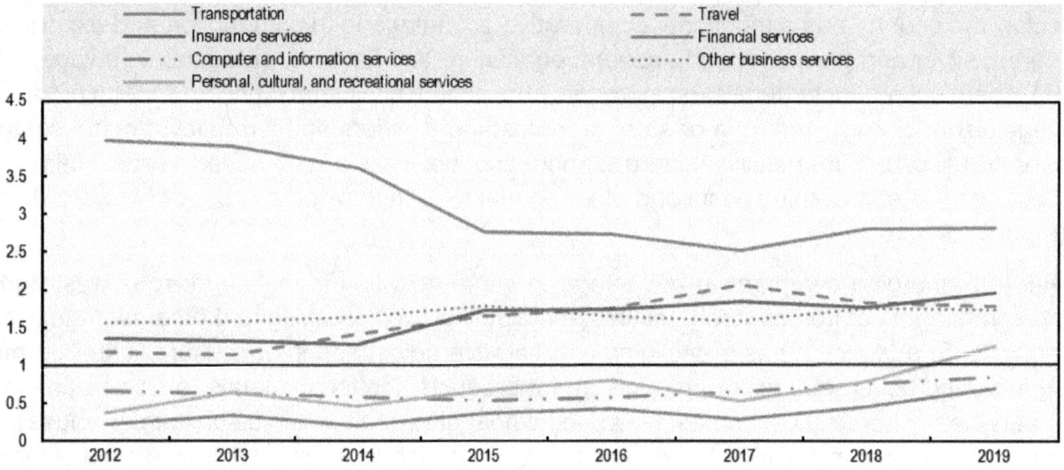

Note: Exports of services are classified according to EBOPS 2002.
Source: OECD elaboration based on UN Comtrade (2022[15]), exports of services, https://comtrade.un.org/data

Box 2.1. Assessing Chile's revealed comparative advantage: methodology and data

The revealed comparative advantage (RCA) measures the relative advantage or disadvantage of a country in a given sector, as evidenced by its trade flows. RCA is based on the Ricardian comparative advantage concept and was introduced by Balassa (1965[16]). It is calculated following the approach of Feenstra (2016[17]) and export data from the UN Comtrade database.

Given that exports of goods and services follow different sector classifications, the RCA analysis is carried out separately. The analysis of exports of goods is carried out for more than 250 sub-sectors in 14 broader sectors classified according to SITC Rev 4 (3-digit). Chile has a RCA in a sector if it exports relatively more in that sector than the rest of the world. Given the high number of sub-sectors, it is useful to classify them into traditional, emerging, declining and marginal:

- **Traditional** subsectors are those in which Chile has had a RCA in at least three years in both five-year periods used in the analysis: 2012-16 and 2017-21. Traditional sub-sectors are thus those in which Chile has traditionally had a comparative advantage in exports.
- **Emerging** sub-sectors are those in which Chile has gained a comparative advantage more recently; that is, Chilean producers had a RCA in at least three years in 2017-21, but in less than three years in 2012-16. Consequently, emerging sectors can be considered as potential new growth pools.
- **Declining** sub-sectors are sectors where Chile has lost comparative advantage in the last decade. These sub-sectors had a comparative advantage in the past, but experienced a RCA in less than three years in 2017-21.
- **Marginal** sub-sectors are those that did not have a RCA in at least three years in both periods. These sectors may therefore be further away from gaining a competitive advantage in Chile.

The analysis for exports of services is based on a smaller group of sub-sectors classified according to (EBOPS 2002) for the period 2012-19. Chile has a comparative advange in a service category if the RCA is above 1 in all years of the 8-year analysis period.

2.2.3. Foreign firms support Chile's exports, including in high-tech and knowledge-intensive sectors

According to the Sexta Encuesta Longitudinal de Empresas (ELE6), in 2019 foreign companies contributed more than 50% of total exports in almost all sectors covered by the survey (Figure 2.11, Panel A). For example, foreign firms were responsible for about 90% of total exports in manufacturing, 85% in finance, 83% in real estate, and 73% in information and communication. The data also show that foreign affiliates accounted for a significant share of exporting firms in many sectors. For instance they represented 64% of all exporting firms in finance, 44% in real estate, and 40% in information and communication (Figure 2.11, Panel B).

The importance of foreign companies for Chile's exports is confirmed by information provided by the Internal Revenue Service of Chile. According to data from the Internal Revenue Service, in 2020 foreign firms contributed more than 50% of total exports in most sectors including knowledge-intensive and high-tech sectors. For example, they accounted for approximately 80% of exports in telecommunications and in information service activities, 55% in computer activities, 50% in electronics, machinery and equipment, and chemicals. Moreover, they also accounted for about 30% of exports in scientific research and development.

Data from the Internal Revenue Service also reveal that foreign companies in Chile are more export-oriented than domestic companies, as they export a larger share of their sales (Figure 2.12). In 2020, in almost all sectors, with the exception of hospitality, health and social work, and energy, foreign firms exported a greater share of their sales than domestic firms. Higher differences between foreign and domestic firms are observed in defence and mining. A regression analysis based on ELE6 confirms the existence of a foreign premium in relation to export intensity regardless of firm size and sector. In particular, the econometric findings show that foreign ownership increases export intensity by 32% (Annex 2.B).

Figure 2.11. Foreign firms contribute significantly to Chilean exports in many sectors

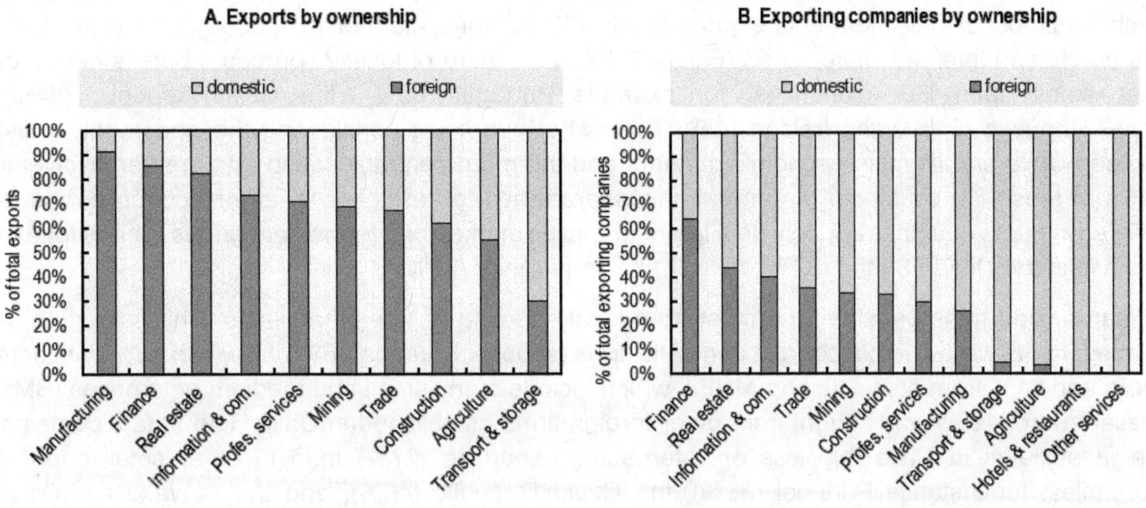

Source: OECD elaboration based on Sexta Encuesta Longitudinal de Empresas (2019[8]), https://www.ine.cl/estadisticas/economia/ciencia-y-tecnologia/encuesta-longitudinal-de-empresas.

Figure 2.12. Foreign affiliates are more export-oriented than Chilean firms

Relative difference between export intensity of foreign and domestic firms (>0 if foreign firms are more export-intensive than domestic firms), 2020

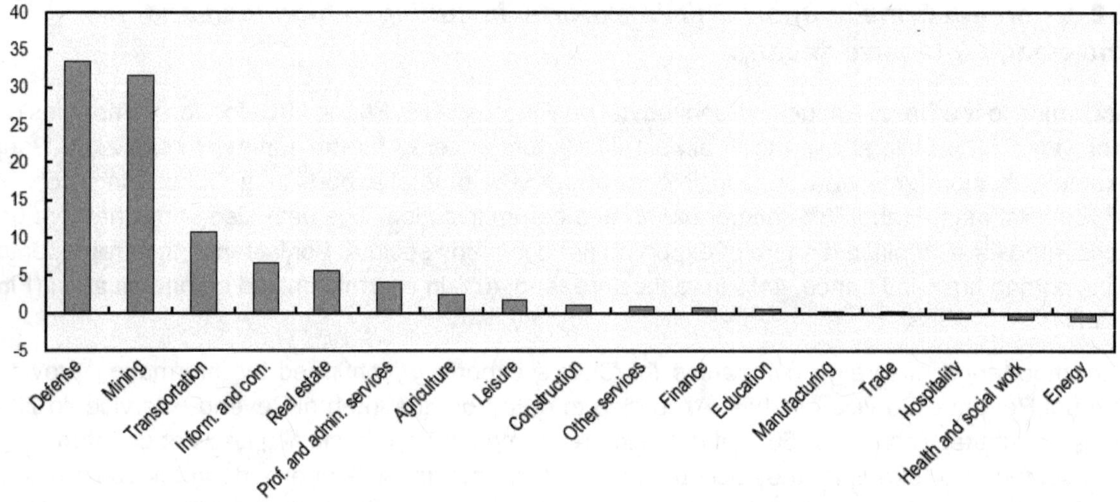

Note: Results are based on a subsample of firms with median sales >= USD 100 000 and median number of workers >= 5. Export intensity: gross exports over sales. The indicator measures the relative difference between export intensity of foreign and domestic firms. Values above 0 indicate that foreign firms are more export oriented than domestic firms and vice versa.
Source: OECD elaboration based on information compiled by the Internal Revenue Service of Chile.

2.2.4. The extent of linkages between foreign and domestic firms is significant

While foreign firms foster integration into GVCs through their import and export activities, their participation in domestic value chains can also contribute to the productivity growth of domestic firms (OECD, forthcoming[18]). In particular, buyer-supplier relationships (so-called value chain linkages) can enable productivity improvements through access to new technologies, knowledge and better or cheaper inputs (Alfaro-Ureña, Manelici and Vasquez, 2022[19]).[3]

Indicators based on the OECD's AMNE analytical database show that, in 2016, foreign firms in Chile purchased most of their intermediate goods locally (73% of total intermediate goods), while a smaller share was purchased internationally (27%) (Figure 2.13). The share of locally sourced inputs is higher than in other small open EU economies, for example Portugal (62%), the Czech Republic (54%), the Slovak Republic (51%), and Ireland (45%)This is not surprising considering the geographical distance between Chile and its main economic partners and the more central location and greater involvement in GVCs of these EU countries. In general, this share tends to be higher in larger economies, as foreign affiliates in those countries can rely on a larger domestic market for intermediate goods. This is for example the case in the United States (82%), Italy (71%) and France (70%).

Chilean-owned firms benefited the most from local sourcing of foreign affiliates. The majority of locally sourced inputs were purchased from domestic firms (supplier linkages): 63%, of which 12% from domestic MNEs and 51% from domestic non-MNEs, which include many small and medium enterprises (SMEs). A smaller share, 10%, was bought from other foreign firms established in Chile. The data also reveal that foreign affiliates in Chile rely less on international sourcing (27%) than in other small open OECD economies, for instance Portugal (38%), the Czech Republic (46%), and the Slovak Republic (48%). Normally, the share of inputs bought internationally tends to be higher in small economies due to their smaller domestic market for intermediate goods.

Figure 2.13. In Chile, foreign firms source inputs mainly from Chilean firms

Sourcing structure of foreign affiliates by country, 2016

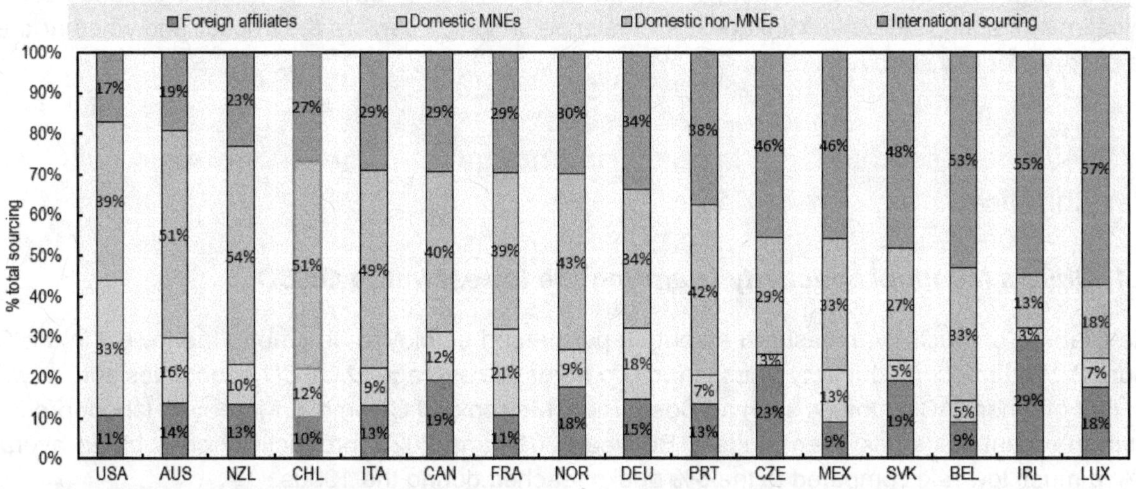

Source: OECD (2018[20]), Analytical AMNE database, https://www.oecd.org/sti/ind/analytical-amne-database.htm.

The indicators also show that in Chile almost 70% of foreign affiliates' output feeds back into domestic value chains. In 2016, 36% of the output of foreign affiliates was used as input by local firms, and 33% was sold in the domestic market for final goods and services (Figure 2.14). The share of foreign affiliates' output that stays in Chile is higher than in other small open economies such as Portugal (60%), the Czech Republic (52%), Ireland (44%), the Slovak Republic (43%) and Belgium (37%).

Figure 2.14. Foreign firms sell intermediate products mainly to Chilean firms

Output use of foreign affiliates, Chile vs other OECD economies, 2016

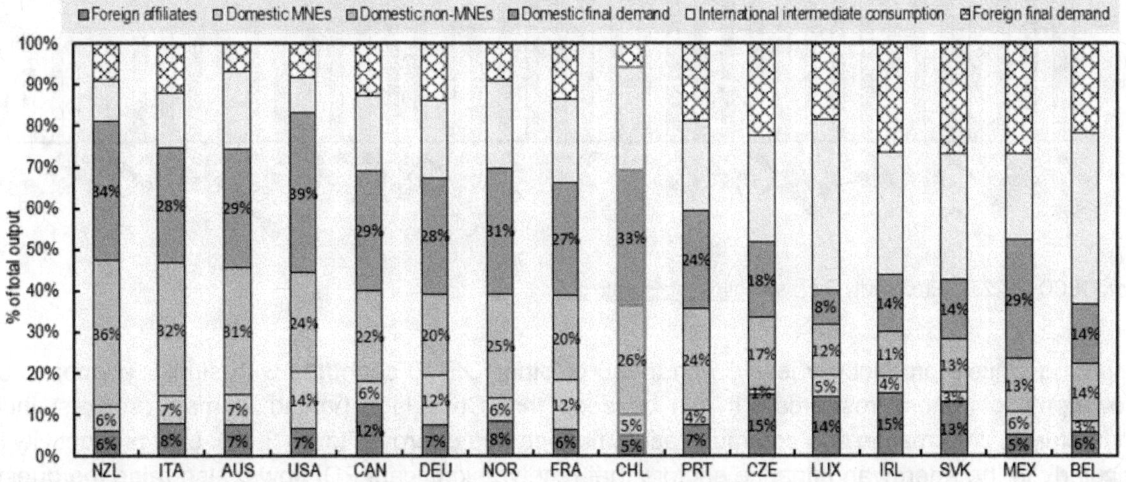

Source: OECD (2018[20]), Analytical AMNE database, https://www.oecd.org/sti/ind/analytical-amne-database.htm.

Moreover, the share of output sold to Chilean firms (buyer linkages) is significant: in 2016, intermediate products sold by foreign affiliates to domestic firms accounted for 31% of their output (26% was sold to non-domestic MNEs and 5% to domestic MNEs), while inputs sold to other foreign firms located in Chile corresponded to 5% of output. The extent of sell linkages is greater in Chile than in other small open economies, for example Portugal (28%), the Czech Republic (18%), Luxembourg (17%) and Ireland (15%). In general, the importance of buyer-supplier linkages in Chile suggests that foreign affiliates are well integrated into the domestic economy. Nonetheless, further analysis is needed to understand the implications of such value chain linkages, for instance, in which sectors they occur and whether they act as a channel for FDI spillovers.

2.3. FDI fosters productivity, innovation and can support economic diversification

2.3.1. Chile's labour productivity is among the lowest in the OECD

Chile's labour productivity, measured as output per person employed, is among the lowest in the OECD (Figure 2.15). Labour productivity is less than two-thirds the average of OECD economies and only higher than that of other LAC countries such as Costa Rica, Mexico and Colombia. Moreover, labour productivity growth in recent years has been modest. Between 2010 and 2020, productivity grew by an average of 0.8%, a much low rate compared to the 5% peaks reached during the 1990s.

Figure 2.15. Chile's labour productivity is among the lowest in the OECD

GDP per person employed, USD, current PPPs, 2020

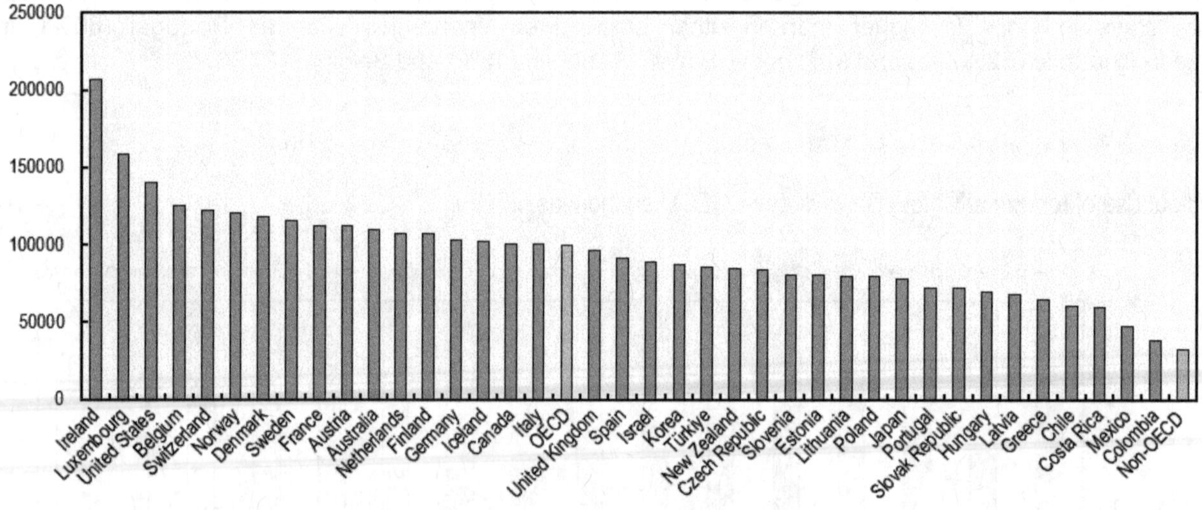

Source: OECD (2022[22]), Productivity Database, https://stats.oecd.org/

Comparing Chile's productivity levels with those of other OECD countries with similar economic size or endowments of natural resources, it can be seen that Chile lags behind in many sectors, including manufacturing, information and communication, finance and energy (Figure 2.16). Low productivity levels, particularly in the energy and finance sectors that receive significant FDI flows, also raise the question of whether domestic firms able to benefit from the positive spillovers of foreign firms.

The low levels of labour productivity in Chile are due to both economic and regulatory factors. Low business investment in R&D and innovation and a fragmented public system for innovation are crucial factors behind Chile's stagnant productivity. Moreover, regulatory barriers create skill imbalances, which reduce productivity and leave many workers in low-wage and temporary jobs (see Chapter 3) (OECD, 2018[22]).

Low productivity is also linked to business polarisation. Chile has a persistent division between a small number of large and productive firms and a long tail of small and medium-sized firms with significantly lower productivity performance. The lack of a cohort of medium-sized enterprises is an obstacle to business dynamism and competitive pressure (OECD, 2021[23]). Regulatory barriers, including market access restrictions, that hinder competition in many key sectors, such as telecommunications, maritime services and railways, also limit the entry of firms and reduce productivity. Chile's low productivity is also linked to the low sophistication of its economy, understood as a wealth of diverse and internationally competitive firms in a wide range of productive sectors (OECD, 2021[23]).

Figure 2.16. Chile's productivity performance is weak in many sectors

Value added per hour worked by activity

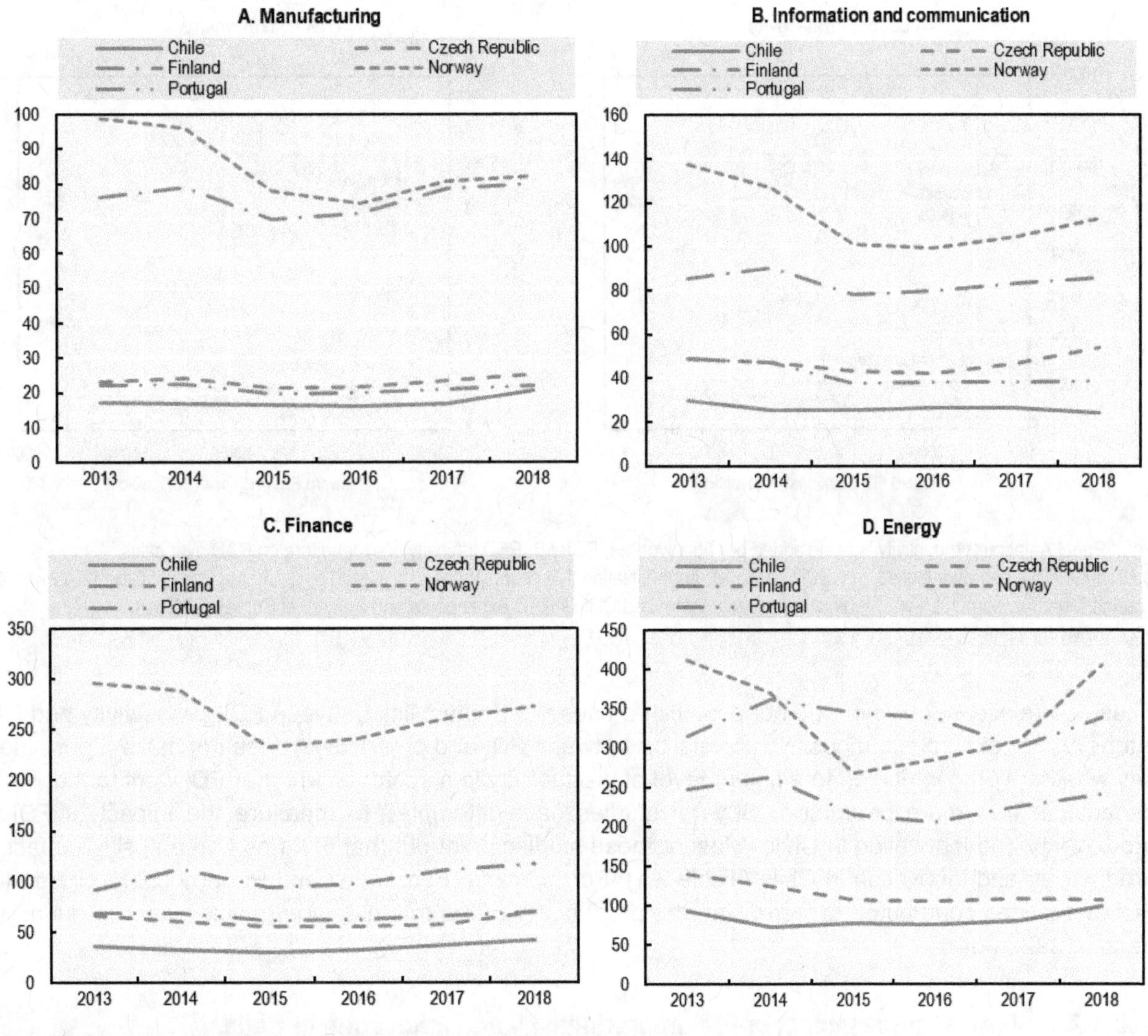

Source: OECD (2022[24]) Annual National Accounts, https://stats.oecd.org/.

2.3.2. FDI is concentrated in capital-intensive and more productive sectors

In Chile, FDI is concentrated in the capital-intensive mining and energy sectors and in financial services, which are relatively more productive, i.e. where an hour of labour produces more value added on average than in other sectors (Figure 2.17, Panel A). Smaller shares of FDI go to sectors with lower average labour productivity levels, such as agriculture, manufacturing, construction, tourism, trade, transport and communications. The exceptions are real estate and business services, which, despite being highly productive, receive a low share of FDI. A positive relationship between FDI and productivity at the aggregate level is not unusual in countries that are important producers of natural resources (OECD, 2019[25]). Sectors that attract more FDI – mining, energy and financial services – have lower R&D intensity, i.e. they spend less on R&D as a percentage of sales, however (Panel B). Conversely, sectors that receive smaller shares of FDI, notably business services and manufacturing, have higher R&D intensity. A negative correlation between FDI and R&D intensity is observed in other natural resource-rich countries (OECD, 2019[25]).

Figure 2.17. FDI is concentrated in sectors that are more productive, but spend less on R&D

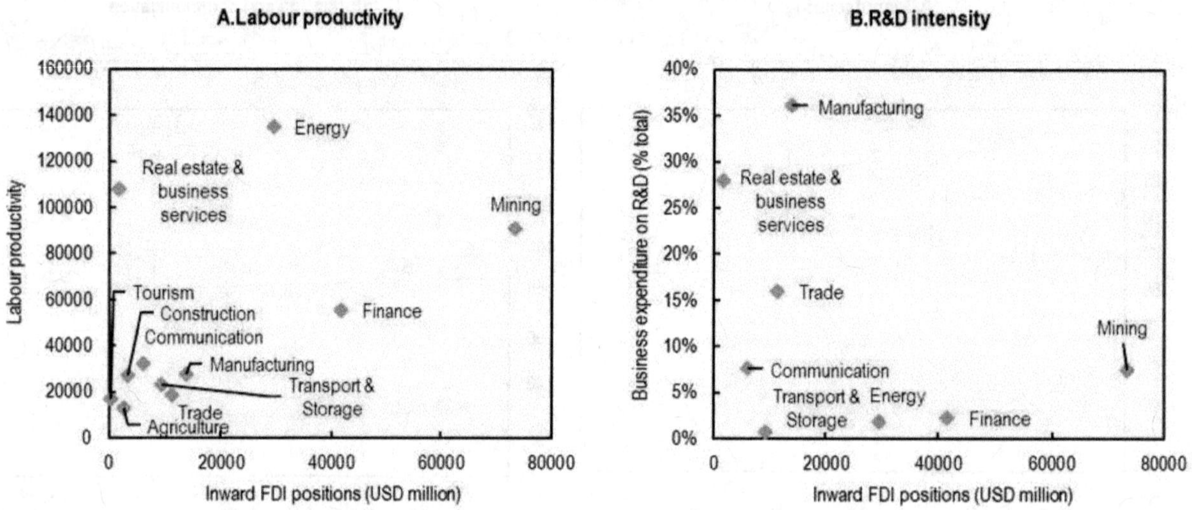

Note: Panel A: labour productivity is value added per hour worked; Panel B: R&D intensity is expenditure on R&D over sales.
Source: OECD elaboration based on OECD (2022[24]), Annual National Accounts, https://stats.oecd.org/; Central Bank of Chile (2022[4]), Foreign Direct Investment, https://www.bcentral.cl/en/home; and Chile's R&D Expenditure and Personnel Survey (2018[26]), https://www.minciencia.gob.cl.

These correlations, however, do not establish a cause-and-effect link between FDI, productivity and R&D intensity. For example, the positive correlation between FDI and productivity does not make it possible to say whether FDI contributed to a higher level of productivity in a sector or whether FDI went to that sector because it was more productive. Several studies have attempted to measure the impact of FDI on productivity and innovation in Chile. Most of these studies point out that FDI has had a positive effect on productivity and innovation in Chile (Table 2.1). For example, Fernandez and Paunov (2012[27]) find that FDI in services contributed to increasing the productivity of the manufacturing sector in Chile during the period 1992-2004.

Table 2.1. Studies on the impact of FDI on productivity and innovation in Chile

Authors	Variable of interest	Main findings
Trojette (2016[28])	GDP growth	FDI enhanced GDP growth during 1984-2013 in countries with good institutional quality, including Chile.
OECD (2015[10])	Labour productivity	Foreign firms in Chile are more productive and capital -intensive than domestic firms.
Ilboudo (2014[29])	Total factor productivity	FDI is positively and significantly correlated with TFP in the mining sector in

Authors	Variable of interest	Main findings
		Chile.
Castillo et al. (2014[30])	Total factor productivity	Using firm-level data for Chilean companies, they find a positive productivity spillovers from FDI.
Fernandez and Paunov (2012[27])	Labour productivity growth	FDI in services significantly and positively affected productivity growth of Chilean manufacturing plants during 1992-2004.
Ramirez (2006[31])	Labour productivity growth	FDI had a positive and economically significant effect on the rate of labour productivity growth in Chile during 1960-2000.
Chowdhury and Mavrotas (2005[32])	GDP growth	They find no relationship between FDI and GDP growth in Chile during 1969-2000.
Alvarez (2001[33])	Technology innovation indicators	FDI increases some technology innovation (e.g. design, packaging) in Chile in the 1990s.

2.3.3. Foreign firms are more productive and engage more in R&D activities

The Sexta Encuesta Longitudinal de Empresas (ELE6) provides information on the performance of foreign and domestic firms in Chile in 2019 (Annex 2.A). Data on sales, cost of intermediate goods and employment are used to calculate firm productivity. Based on this information, an indicator is constructed that measures the relative productivity gap between foreign and domestic firms. The indicator shows that foreign firms have a productivity premium in most sectors (Figure 2.18, Panel A). Such premium is particularly high in trade, construction, mining, manufacturing and energy. When comparing large firms (84% of foreign firms and 39% of domestic firms), productivity gaps narrow significantly or disappear. [4]

In most sectors, foreign firms are also more likely to engage in R&D activities than domestic firms (Panel B).[5] Among the few exceptions, the mining sector is an interesting case, given the significant share of FDI attracted and the capital intensity of the sector. The lower R&D propensity of foreign mining firms could be explained by the fact that these firms carry out R&D in other countries, e.g. in their home country or closer to major R&D centres. Moreover, when comparing large companies, the gaps narrow with a few exceptions.

Additional empirical analysis confirms the existence of a foreign premium in relation to productivity (Annex 2.B). The analysis allows to single out the impact of foreign ownership on firm's performance by taking into account factors such as size and sector. The results show that foreign ownership is positively and significantly correlated with productivity, regardless of size and sector. In particular, foreign ownership has an impact of about 80% on firm productivity (i.e. increases firm productivity by 80%). These results are overall consistent with the predictions of economic theory: due to the sunk costs of investing abroad, foreign firms are on average more productive and export more intensively than purely domestic firms export more intensively than purely domestic firms (Melitz, 2003[36]; Helpman, Melitz and Yeaple, 2004[37]).

Figure 2.18. Foreign firms are more productive and are more likely to engage in R&D activities

Relative gap between foreign and domestic firms (if >0 foreign firms are more productive/engage more in R&D activities than domestic firms)

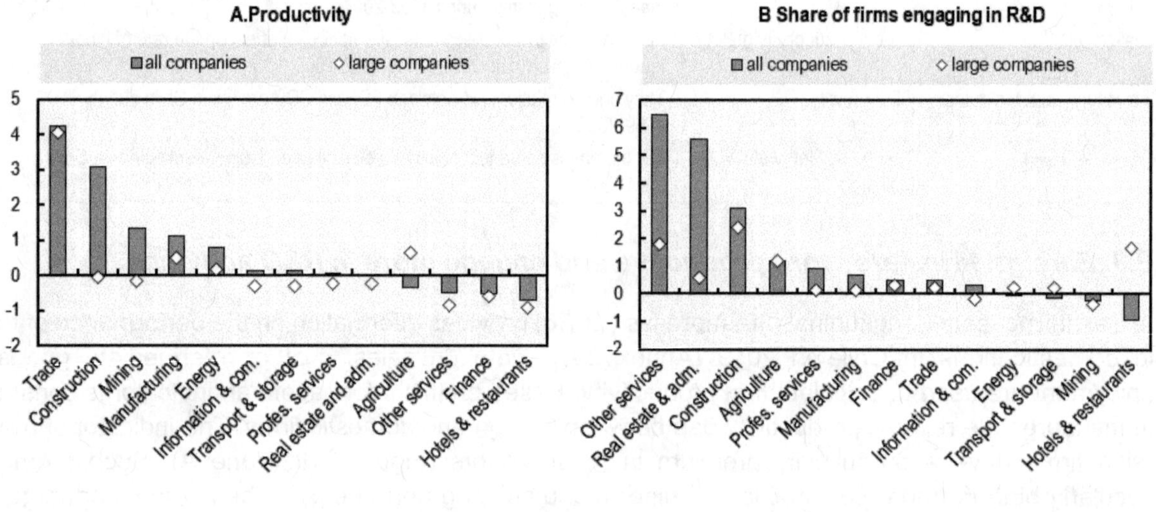

Note: Labour productivity is value added per hour worked. Productivity data refer to 2019, R&D data to 2017. Large companies are companies whose sales exceed 100 001 UF. Firms engaging in R&D are firms with positive expenditure on R&D. The indicators in Panel A and B show the relative gap between foreign and domestic firms, e.g. (productivity of foreign firms – productivity of domestic firms)/ productivity of domestic firms. Positive values indicate that foreign firms perform better (e.g. are more productive) than domestic firms and vice versa. The indicators are calculated for all companies and for large companies only.
Source: OECD elaboration based on fDi Markets (2022[6]), greenfield FDI, https://www.fdimarkets.com/.

2.3.4. Foreign firms can enhance the economic diversification of the Chilean economy

Diversifying the economy away from natural resource activities has been a long-term goal for Chile. Since the 1970s, with different emphasis, policies have sought to strengthen the role of the private sector and increase the sophistication of exports. Although these policies have helped diversify Chile's production base and export basket, economic activity is still largely concentrated in the primary sector (mining, agriculture and fishery), low value-added manufacturing and services (e.g. public sector). Dependence on the export of raw materials, especially copper, and the lack of a strong policy framework for innovation/research, development, and human capital development, as well as some regulatory barriers, have contributed to hindering further economic diversification towards high-tech and knowledge-intensive activities.

As shown earlier in this chapter, foreign investment in Chile is also concentrated in a few sectors. These are natural resources (mining and energy), finance, trade and medium and low-tech manufacturing industries (food, chemicals). Foreign investors have traditionally been attracted by the country's vast endowment of natural resources, particularly metals (copper) and coal. More recently, Chile's commitment to a green transition has created the basis for attracting foreign capital to green energy industries. Chile's environmental goals and its unique geography, making it one of the countries in the world with the highest potential for renewable energy development, explain the increasing share of FDI in renewable energy projects. Beyond natural resources, however, foreign investors favour a small number of sectors where they can rely on well-developed domestic capacities, including existing pools of local suppliers and expertise (Figure 2.19).

Figure 2.19. There is potential to enhance FDI diversification

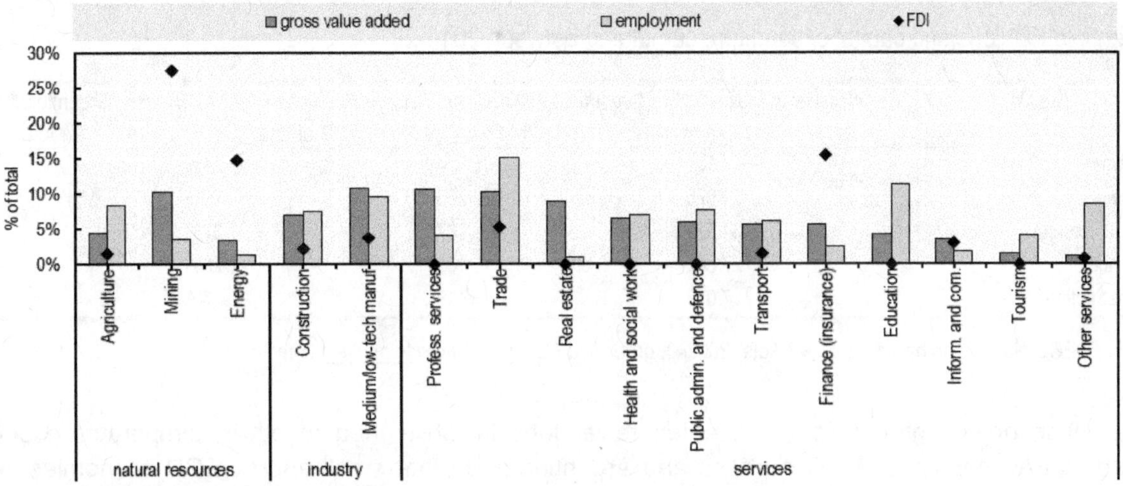

Note: About 24% of FDI are 'not allocated', thus some sectoral shares may be underestimated.
Source: OECD elaboration based on OECD (2022[24]), Annual National Accounts, https://stats.oecd.org/, Central Bank of Chile (2022[4]), Foreign Direct Investment, https://www.bcentral.cl/en/home.

Attracting FDI in a larger range of sectors, especially high-tech and knowledge intensive sectors, can help Chile become a more diversified, resilient and knowledge-intensive economy. Foreign firms have access to better technologies and can disseminate them in the host economy. They can also act as a gateway to international markets and foster integration into GVCs. The results presented earlier in this chapter show that foreign firms are more likely to engage in innovation activities and contribute significantly to exports, including in high-tech and knowledge-intensive sectors. Foreign firms are on average more productive than domestic firms, thus contributing positively to the productivity of the sector in which they directly operate. At the same time, foreign firms can help the domestic economy to become more productive through spillovers to domestic firms, i.e. through the transfer of technology and knowledge. The analysis presented in the chapter highlights the presence of significant linkages in the value chain between foreign and Chilean firms, which can be an important channel for FDI spillover.

Attracting more FDI in high-tech manufacturing and knowledge-intensive sectors requires co-ordinated policy action by various institutions, particularly with regard to FDI promotion and facilitation, innovation/R&D policies, and skills policies. Chapter 3 analyses Chile's policy framework for productivity, innovation and skills development in depth and provides policy guidance on how to exploit opportunities brought by foreign investment.

2.4. FDI promotes a more quality jobs and green economy

2.4.1. FDI is directed to sectors with less potential for job creation

Between 2010 and 2020, greenfield FDI in Chile generated more than 106 000 jobs (Table 2.2). About 34% of these jobs were created in mining and energy, a rather small share considering that almost two-thirds of greenfield FDI went to these sectors. About 32% of jobs were created in manufacturing, 26% in services and 7% in construction. These shares are significant given that only a quarter of greenfield investments went to these sectors (10% in manufacturing, 19% in services and 1% in construction). Although these data provide only a partial picture of the employment impact of FDI in Chile, as they do not take into account jobs created through mergers and acquisitions (M&A) and expansion projects, they indicate that a large share of FDI is directed towards sectors with less potential for job creation.

Table 2.2. Between 2010 and 2020, about 32% of jobs created by greenfield FDI were in manufacturing

Greenfield FDI jobs and capital expenditure cumulated between 2010-20

Sector	Number of jobs	Greenfield FDI (million USD)	Jobs (% of total)	Greenfield FDI (% total)
Energy	15 131	35 884	14%	44%
Mining	21 675	22 395	20%	27%
Manufacturing	34 532	7 767	32%	10%
Services	27 847	15 182	26%	19%
Construction	7 076	419	7%	1%

Source: OECD elaboration based on fDi Markets (2022[6]), greenfield FDI, https://www.fdimarkets.com/.

One million dollars greenfield FDI creates fewer jobs in Chile than in other comparator economies, including LAC countries like Costa Rica and Argentina and other small open OECD economies such as the Czech Republic, Poland and Portugal (Figure 2.20). In these comparator countries, an important share of FDI is directed towards manufacturing, services and construction, sectors with higher employment potential. For instance, between 2010 and 2020, about 50% of all jobs created by greenfield FDI in Costa Rica were in the IT and business services and medical devices, which receive about a quarter of greenfield FDI. At the same time, the number of jobs created by greenfield FDI in Chile is similar to that created in other natural resource-rich countries, notably Australia and Norway, which also receive significant shares of greenfield investments in mining and energy.

Information collected by the Chile's Internal Revenue Service shows that foreign firms contribute significantly to employment in all sectors of the economy (Figure 2.21). Unsurprisingly, the contribution to employment is greatest in sectors that receive a higher amount of FDI. In 2020, foreign firms were responsible for about 50% of employment in mining and 44% in finance, sectors that receive important shares of FDI (28% mining and 15% finance according to Central Bank of Chile' data). A significant contribution to employment is also observed in hospitality (41%), information and communication (35%) and energy (35%), while smaller shares are found in education (18%), defence (16%), agriculture (14%) and construction (14%).

Figure 2.20. Greenfield FDI creates less jobs in Chile than in other peers

Jobs created by 1 million dollar greenfield FDI between 2010-20 by sector

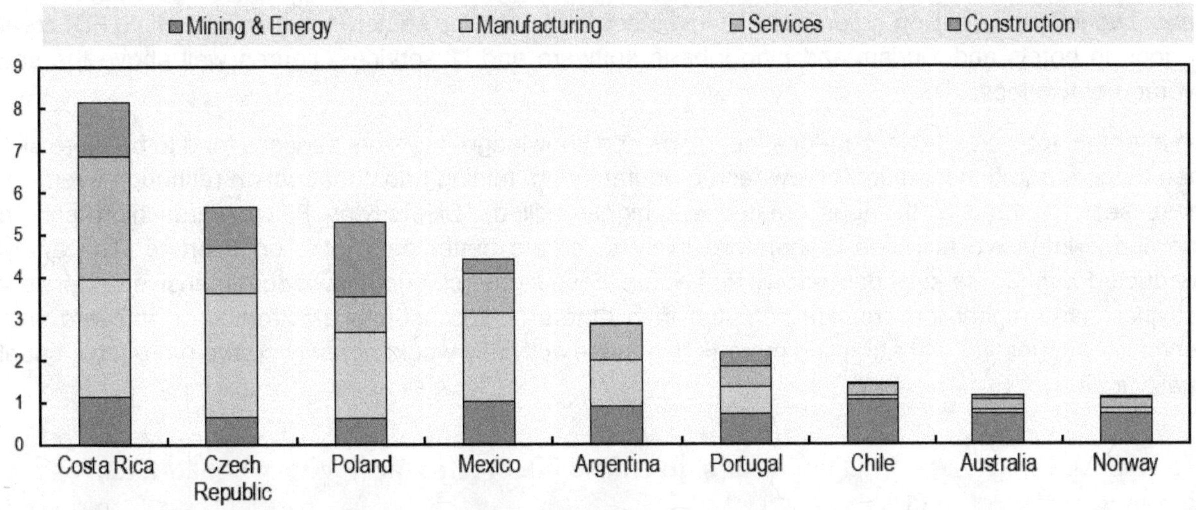

Source: OECD elaboration based on fDi Markets (2022[6]), greenfield FDI, https://www.fdimarkets.com/.

Figure 2.21. Foreign firms contribute significantly to employment in all sectors

Number of employees by firm ownership (% of total), 2020

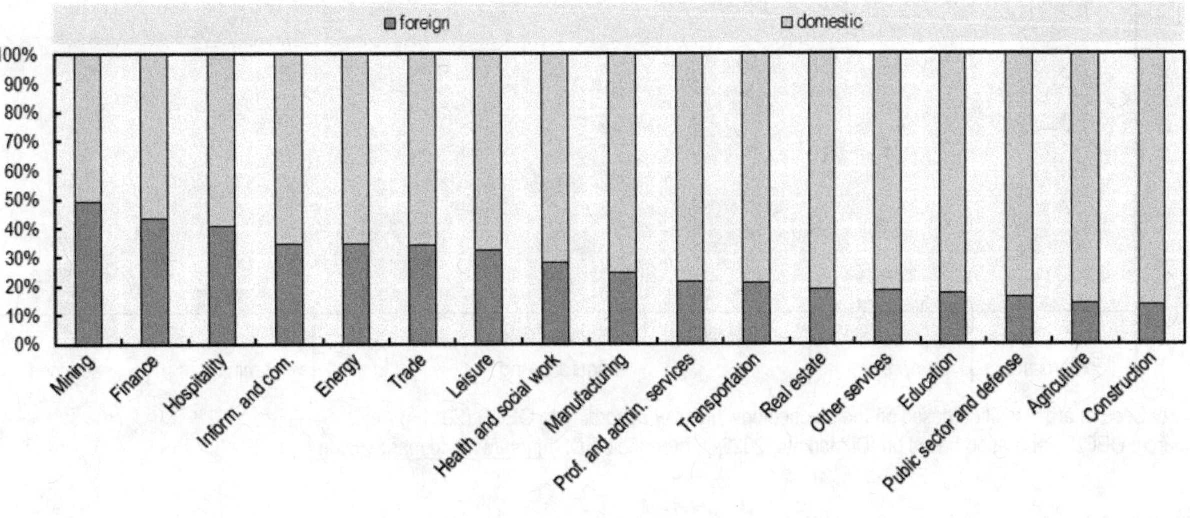

Note: Results are based on a subsample of firms with median sales >= USD 100 000 and median number of workers >= 5.
Source: OECD elaboration based on information compiled by the Internal Revenue Service of Chile.

2.4.2. Attracting FDI into high-tech manufacturing and knowledge-intensive services can create better quality jobs

A closer look at the data shows that 1 million dollars greenfield FDI invested in Chile between 2010 and 2021 created the most jobs in the construction sector (around 17 jobs per million greenfield FDI invested), followed by high-tech manufacturing (9), low-tech manufacturing (4) and medium-tech manufacturing (4) (Figure 2.22). Relatively fewer jobs were created in services (2), mining (1) and energy (less than 1). These aggregate figures hide large heterogeneity within sectors, however. For example, in high-tech manufacturing, 1 million greenfield FDI invested created about 20 jobs in consumer electronics, but only two jobs in biotechnology (Annex 2.C). In medium-tech manufacturing, the highest number of jobs was generated in automotive components, nine jobs, while the lowest number was created in building materials, about two jobs for 1 million greenfield FDI invested. In the service sector, 1 million greenfield FDI created 13 jobs in hotels and tourism and nine jobs in software and IT services, figures well above the sector average of two jobs.

On average, jobs created in high-tech industries and knowledge-intensive services tend to be more skilled than those created in medium- or low-tech manufacturing, mining and construction (although even within these sectors some of the jobs created are highly skilled). Diversifying FDI towards high-tech- and knowledge-intensive activities is therefore likely to create better paid jobs, on average. The analysis conducted with fDi Markets' data shows that within these high-tech and knowledge-intensive sectors some activities have higher job creation potential than others (e.g. consumer electronics or software and IT services), suggesting that attracting more FDI in these activities would not only create more jobs, but also quality jobs.

Figure 2.22. On average, 1 million dollars greenfield FDI creates more jobs in construction and high-tech manufacturing

Jobs created per million dollars greenfield FDI invested by sector

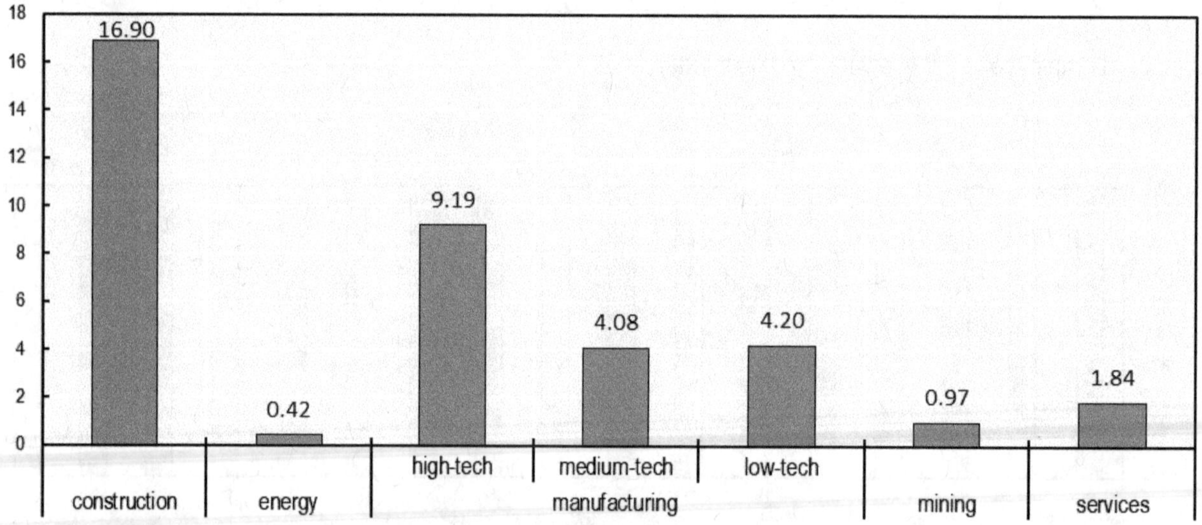

Note: Sectors are classified based on their technology intensity according to OECD (2011[5])
Source: OECD elaboration based on fDi Markets (2022[6]), greenfield FDI, https://www.fdimarkets.com/.

2.4.3. Foreign companies offer better paid and more skill-intensive jobs, including for women

Earlier parts of this report show that foreign companies are on average more productive than Chilean companies. The higher productivity of foreign companies is explained by the fact that they have access to better technology of the parent company. Higher productivity can translate into higher average wages for workers. In addition, the use of more advanced technologies may induce the foreign company to hire more skilled employees or to invest more in training to enable employees to learn or keep up with those technologies.

Analysis based on ELE6 shows that, on average, foreign companies pay higher wages than domestic companies in most sectors (Figure 2.23, Panel A). Interestingly, this result holds even if only large firms are compared.[6] These wage premia are particularly high in construction, trade and manufacturing. The results also show that foreign firms tend to have higher shares of skilled workers than domestic firms in all sectors, particularly in energy, construction and mining (Panel B). These premia persist if only large firms are considered.

Figure 2.23. Foreign firms pay higher wages and are more skill-intensive than domestic firms

Relative gap between foreign and domestic firms (if >0 foreign firms pay higher wages/are more skill intensive than domestic firms)

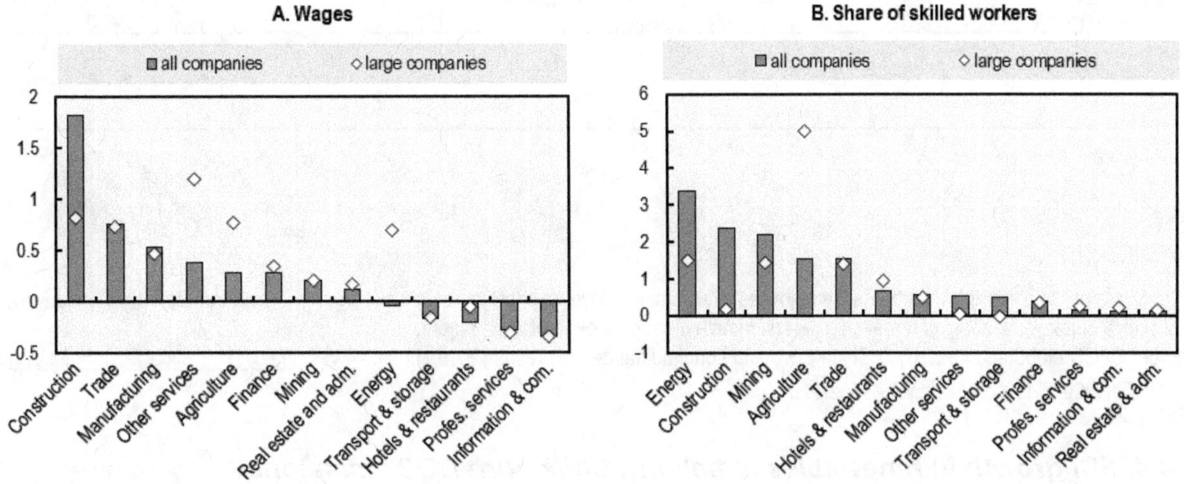

Note: Panel A: Wages: labour costs divided by total number of employees. Panel B: Skilled employees are employees with a university degree or higher. The indicators in Panel A and B show the relative gap between foreign and domestic firms, e.g. (wages of foreign firms – wages of domestic firms)/ wages of domestic firms. Positive values indicate that foreign firms perform better (e.g. pay higher wages) than domestic firms and vice versa. The indicators are calculated for all companies and for large companies only.
Source: OECD elaboration based on Sexta Encuesta Longitudinal de Empresas (2019[8]), https://www.ine.cl/estadisticas/economia/ciencia-y-tecnologia/encuesta-longitudinal-de-empresas.

The results also show that foreign firms employ higher shares of women than domestic companies in most sectors (Figure 2.24). They tend to employ higher shares of women in energy, transport and storage, and construction, which are typically male-dominated. Moreover, foreign companies have higher shares of skilled female workers (with a university degree or higher) than domestic companies in all sectors. The gap with domestic firms is particularly high in the male-dominated energy and construction sectors, as well as in trade and manufacturing. At the same time, foreign companies have a higher share of female managers than domestic companies in only a few sectors, namely transport and storage, construction, information and communication, and professional services.

An econometric model similar to that used for productivity and export intensity is used to examine whether these foreign premia with respect to employment practices are statistically significant, after controlling for factors such as sector and firm size (Annex 2.B). The analysis shows that foreign ownership has a positive and significant impact on wages, skill intensity and the share of skilled workers, regardless of sector and firm size. In particular, foreign ownership has an impact of about 70% on wages (i.e. foreign firms pay on average 70% higher wages than domestic firms), 88% on skill intensity and 66% on skilled female workers. On the other hand, foreign ownership does not have a significant impact on female employment and the share of female managers, once factors such as sector and company size are controlled for.

Figure 2.24. Foreign firms positively contribute to several gender equality outcomes

Relative gap between foreign and domestic firms (if >0 foreign firms have higher shares of female employees/skilled female employees/female managers than domestic firms)

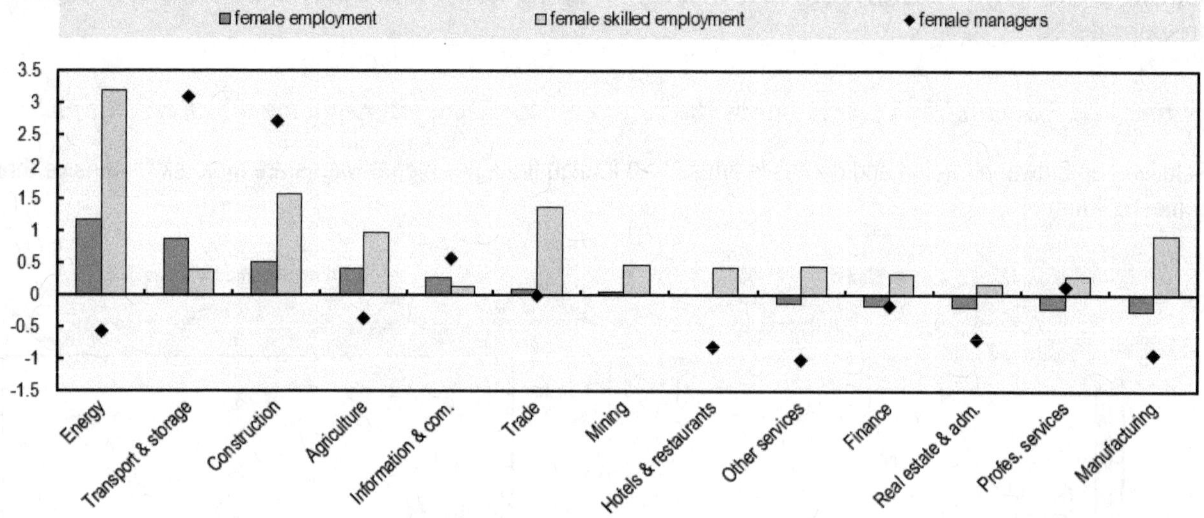

Note: Share of female employees: female employees over total employees; share of female skilled employees: female skilled employees over total skilled employees; share of female managers: female managers over total managers.
Source: OECD elaboration based on Sexta Encuesta Longitudinal de Empresas (2019[8]), https://www.ine.cl/estadisticas/economia/ciencia-y-tecnologia/encuesta-longitudinal-de-empresas.

2.4.4. FDI growth in renewables is helping Chile curb CO2 emissions

In the past three decades, the level of carbon emissions per unit of output in Chile has been similar to that of the average of OECD countries (Figure 2.25, Panel A). However, while carbon emissions as a percentage of GDP in the average of OECD countries have decreased, they have remained stable in Chile. As a result the divergence between the average of OECD countries and Chile has gradually increased since 2008. During the same period, carbon emissions of the average of non-OECD countries, although higher as a percentage of GDP, have also decreased. The combustion of oil products and coal has been responsible for more than 80% of the carbon emissions generated in Chile over the last decades (IEA, 2022[38]). From a sectoral perspective, electricity and heat production and transport account for the bulk of emissions in Chile: over 70% of all carbon emissions in 2020 (Panel B). These shares are similar to those of other comparator countries.

When divided among end-users, manufacturing industry and construction are responsible for the largest share of carbon emissions from electricity and heat use (60%), followed by the residential sector (20%) and services (15%) (Figure 2.26, Panel A). As emissions from heat account for a minor share, increased reliance on clean energy sources for electricity generation and electrification of the transport sector can lead to significant emission reductions. The rapidly falling costs associated with these technologies open up investment opportunities for the private sector, including foreign companies. The sectoral distribution of greenfield FDI flows in Chile shows an important participation of foreign companies in the electricity sector. In particular, between 2010 and 2020, about 47% of greenfield FDI flows were directed to electricity generation (Figure 2.26, Panel B).

Figure 2.25. Chile's CO2 emissions as a share of GDP have been constant over time

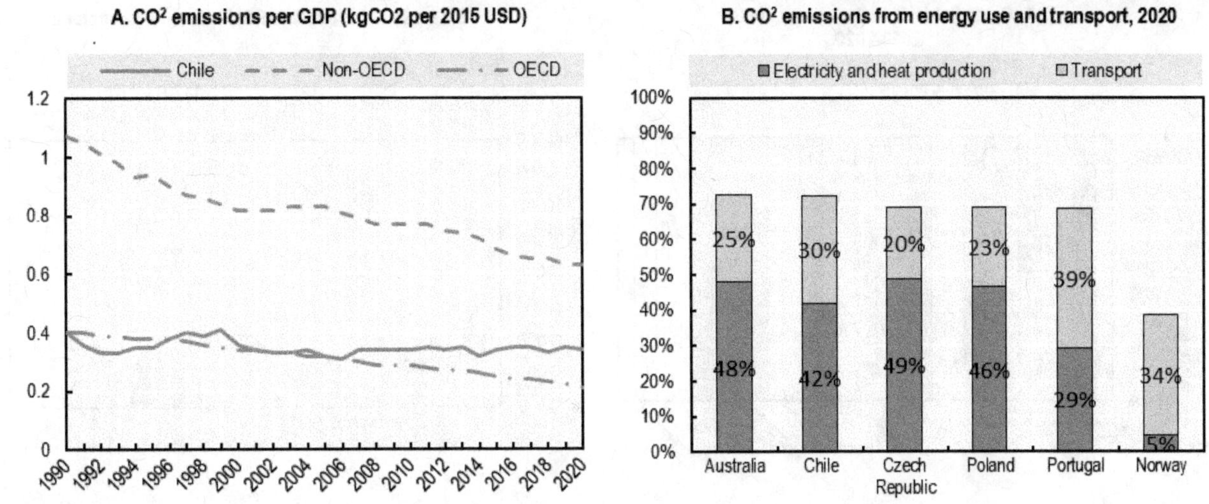

Source: OECD elaboration based on International Energy Agency (IEA) (2022[38]), CO² emissions, https://www.iea.org/

The impact of foreign investors on Chile's carbon footprint depends on whether they promote a shift towards renewable energy. Greenfield FDI data show that between 2010 and 2020, around 88% of greenfield investment flows in Chile's energy sector went to renewable energy, suggesting that foreign companies contribute to the reduction of carbon emissions (Figure 2.27, Panel A). A similar share of greenfield investment in renewable energy is observed in other small open OECD economies, notably Portugal, Costa Rica and Poland, while a higher share is observed in natural resource-rich economies such as Norway and Australia. Furthermore, greenfield investment in renewable energy in Chile has grown significantly over the last decade, while investment in fossil fuels has declined (Figure 2.27, Panel B).

Figure 2.26. Foreign companies invest significantly in electricity generation in Chile

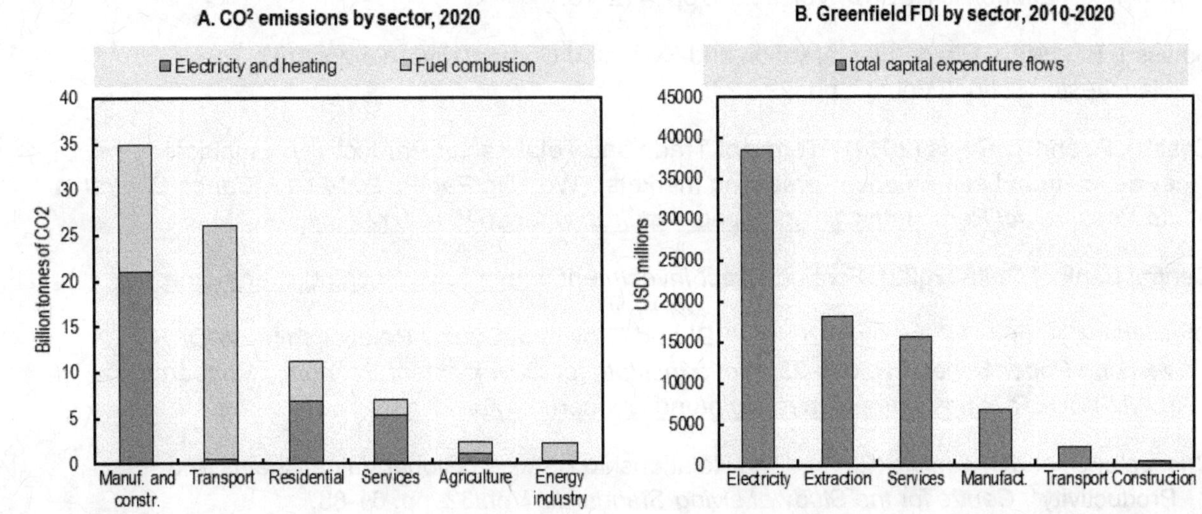

Note: Residential: an energy-consuming sector that consists of living quarters for private households. Common uses of energy associated with this sector include space heating, water heating, air conditioning, lighting, refrigeration, cooking, and running a variety of other appliances.
Source: OECD elaboration based on International Energy Agency (IEA) (2022[38]), CO² emissions, https://www.iea.org/; and fDi Markets (2022[6]), greenfield FDI, https://www.fdimarkets.com/.

Figure 2.27. The bulk of greenfield FDI in Chile's energy sector goes to renewables

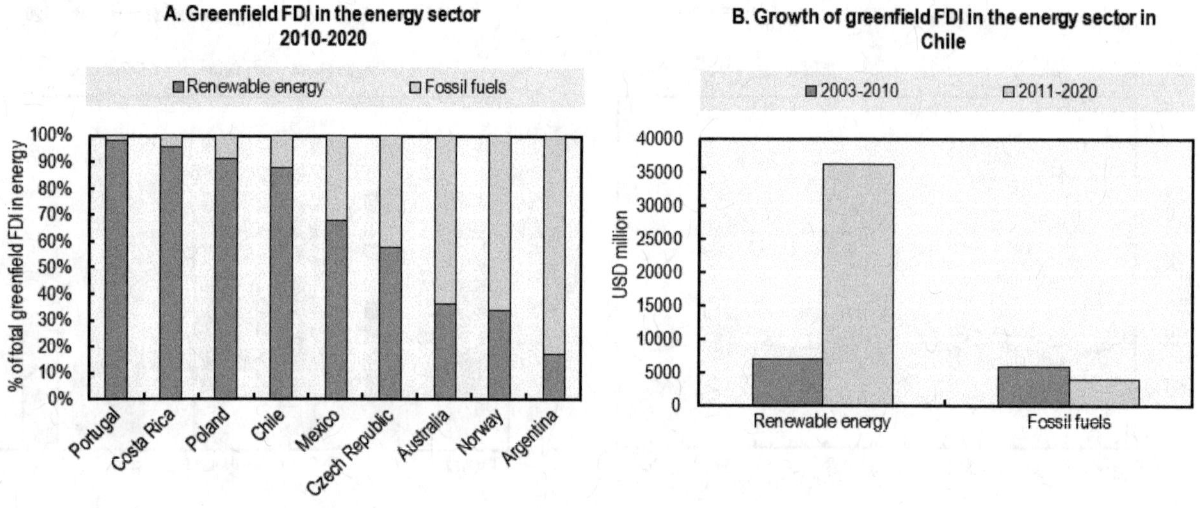

Source: OECD elaboration based on fDi Markets (2022[6]), greenfield FDI, https://www.fdimarkets.com/.

References

Alfaro-Ureña, A., I. Manelici and J. Vasquez (2022), "Linkages, The Effects of Joining Multinational Supply Chains: New Evidence from Firm-to-Firm", *The Quarterly Journal of Economics*, Vol. 137/3, pp. 1495–1552, https://doi.org/10.1093/qje/qjac006. [20]

Alvarez, R. (2001), "External Sources of Technological Innovation", *Estudios de Economía*, Vol. 28/1, pp. 53-68, http://file:///C:/Users/Montinari_L/Downloads/Dialnet-ExternalSourcesOfTechonologicalInnovationInChilean-3279283.pdf. [34]

Antràs, P. et al. (2012), "Measuring the Upstreamness of Production and Trade Flows", *American Economic Review*, Vol. 102/3, pp. 412-16. [13]

Balassa, B. (1965), "Trade Liberalisation and Revealed Comparative Advantage", *The Manchester School*, Vol. 33, pp. 99-123. [16]

Castillo, P. and Y. Rojas (2014), "Terms of Trade and Total Factor Productivity: Empirical evidence from Latin American emerging markets", *Working Papers 2014-012, Banco Central de Reserva del Perú.*, https://ideas.repec.org/p/rbp/wpaper/2014-012.html. [31]

Central Bank of Chile (2022), *Foreign Direct Investment*, https://www.bcentral.cl/en/home. [4]

Chowdhury, A. and G. Mavrotas (2005), "FDI and Growth: a Causal Relationship", *WIDER Working Paper Series RP2005-25, World Institute for Development Economic Research (UNU-WIDER)*, https://ideas.repec.org/p/unu/wpaper/rp2005-25.html. [33]

Criscuolo, C. and J. Timmis (2017), "The Relationship Between Global Value Chains and Productivity", *Centre for the Study of Living Standards*, Vol. 32, pp. 61-83, https://www.oecd.org/global-forum-productivity/events/Relashionship_btween_GVCs_and_productivity_6_09_2016.pdf. [12]

fDi Markets (2022), *Database of crossborder greenfield investments*, https://www.fdimarkets.com/. [6]

Feenstra, R. (2016), "Advanced international trade: Theory and evidence (Second Edition)", *Princeton University Press*. [17]

Fernandes, A. and C. Paunov (2012), "Foreign direct investment in services and manufacturing productivity: Evidence for Chile", *Journal of Development Economics*, Vol. 97/2, pp. 305-321, https://www.sciencedirect.com/science/article/pii/S0304387811000241. [28]

Gonzalez, A. (2017), *3 challenges Latin American economies must overcome to boost intraregional trade*, https://blogs.worldbank.org/trade/3-challenges-latin-american-economies-must-overcome-boost-intraregional-trade. [9]

Government of Chile, Ministry of Science, Technology, Knowledge and Innovation (2018), *Encuesta de Gasto y Personal en I+D (2018)*, https://www.minciencia.gob.cl/areas-de-trabajo/estudios-y-estadisticas/encuesta-sobre-gasto-y-personal-en-investigacion-y-desarrollo-id-ano-2018/. [27]

Government of Chile, The National Institute of Statistics and the Ministry of the Economy (2019), *Encuesta Longitudinal de Empresas 6 (ELE6)*, https://www.ine.cl/estadisticas/economia/ciencia-y-tecnologia/encuesta-longitudinal-de-empresas. [18]

Helpman, E., M. Melitz and S. Yeaple (2004), "Export Versus FDI with Heterogeneous Firms", *American Economic Review*, Vol. 94/1, pp. 300-316, https://www.aeaweb.org/articles?id=10.1257/000282804322970814. [36]

IEA (2022), *Greenhouse Gas Emissions from Energy Data Explorer: Chile*, https://www.iea.org/data-and-statistics/data-tools/greenhouse-gas-emissions-from-energy-data-explorer. [37]

Ilboudo, P. (2014), "Foreign Direct Investment and Total Factor Productivity in The Mining Sector: the Case of Chile", *Economics Honors Papers, Connecticut College*, https://digitalcommons.conncoll.edu/cgi/viewcontent.cgi?article=1015&context=econhp. [30]

Javorcik, B. (2004), "Does Foreign Direct Investment Increase the Productivity of Domestic Firms? In Search of Spillovers Through Backward Linkages", *Americal Economic Review*, Vol. 94/3, pp. 605-627. [38]

Jindra, B. (2006), "The Theoretical Framework: FDI and Technology Transfer", in *Technology Transfer via Foreign Direct Investment in Central and Eastern Europe*, Palgrave Macmillan UK, London, https://doi.org/10.1057/9780230524484_2. [39]

Melitz, M. (2003), "The Impact of Trade on Intra-Industry Reallocations and Aggregate Industry Productivity", *Econometrica*, Vol. 71/6, pp. 1695-1725, https://www.jstor.org/stable/1555536?seq=1#metadata_info_tab_contents. [35]

OECD (2022), *Annual National Accounts*, https://stats.oecd.org/. [25]

OECD (2022), *Explanatory notes on OECD FDI statistics*, https://www.oecd.org/daf/inv/FDI-statistics-explanatory-notes.pdf. [40]

OECD (2022), *FDI Statistics*, https://stats.oecd.org/. [3]

OECD (2022), *Productivity Database*, https://stats.oecd.org/. [22]

OECD (2021), *OECD Economic Surveys: Chile 2021*, https://doi.org/10.1787/79b39420-en. [24]

OECD (2021), *TiVA indicators: 2021 edition*, https://www.oecd.org/sti/ind/measuring-trade-in-value-added.htm. [14]

OECD (2019), *FDI Qualities Indicators: Measuring the sustainable development impacts of investment*, https://www.oecd.org/fr/investissement/fdi-qualities-indicators.htm. [26]

OECD (2018), *Analytical AMNE database*, https://www.oecd.org/sti/ind/analytical-amne-database.htm. [21]

OECD (2018), "Chile Policy Brief: Labour Productivity", https://www.oecd.org/chile/Chile-Boosting-Inclusive-Growth-EN.pdf. [23]

OECD (2015), *Diagnostics of Chile's engagement in Global Value Chains*, https://www.oecd.org/investment/diagnostic-chile-gvc-2015.pdf. [10]

OECD (2011), *Classification of manufacturing industries into categories based on R&D intensities*, https://www.oecd.org/sti/ind/48350231.pdf. [5]

OECD (forthcoming), *"Enabling FDI diffusion channels to boost SME productivity and innovation in EU countries and regions: Towards a Policy Toolkit", OECD DAF-CFE concept paper*. [19]

OECD (Forthcoming), *The geography of foreign investment in OECD countries: how investment promotion agencies support regional development"*. [8]

Ramirez, M. (2006), "Economic and Institutional Determinants of Foreign Direct Investment in Chile: A Time Series Analysis 1960-2001", *Contemporary Economic Policy*, Vol. 24/3, pp. 459-471, http://www.sciepub.com/reference/68328. [32]

Sutherland, D., A. El-Gohari and B. Matthews (2010), *An Exploration of how Chinese Companies Use Tax Havens and Offshore Financial Centres: 'round-tripping' Or 'capital-augmenting' OFDI?*, https://www.oxfordtmcd.org/publication/exploration-how-chinese-companies-use-tax-havens-and-offshore-financial-centres-round. [11]

Thomson Reuters (2022), *M&A Database*, https://legal.thomsonreuters.com/en/products/practical-law/corporate-mergers-and-acquisitions. [7]

Trojette, J. (2016), "The Effect of Foreign Direct Investment on Economic Growth: The Institutional Threshold", *Région et Développement*, Vol. 43, https://regionetdeveloppement.univ-tln.fr/wp-content/uploads/5_Trojette.pdf. [29]

UN Comtrade (2022), *Database*, https://comtrade.un.org/data. [15]

UNCTAD (2021), *World Investment Report*, https://unctad.org/webflyer/world-investment-report-2021. [2]

UNCTAD (2018), *World Investment Report*, https://unctad.org/system/files/official-document/wir2018_en.pdf. [1]

Annex 2.A. Sectoral distribution of Chilean and foreign companies in ELE6

ELE6 covers 4 006 Chilean and 391 foreign companies. Chilean companies are concentrated in trade, real estate and administrative services, professional services, and manufacturing. Foreign companies are prevalent in trade, professional services, and finance. Sampling weights provided by ELE6 are used to calculate statistics and indicators as well as in the regression analysis.

Annex Table 2.A.1. Number and percentage of companies in ELE6 by ownership and sector of activity

	Foreign companies		**Domestic companies**	
Sector	*number*	*percentage*	*number*	*percentage*
Agriculture	7	2%	303	8%
Mining	16	4%	132	3%
Manufacturing	36	9%	407	10%
Energy	11	3%	42	1%
Construction	9	2%	281	7%
Trade	116	30%	1032	26%
Transport & storage	16	4%	227	6%
Hotels & restaurants	4	1%	84	2%
Information & communication	20	5%	120	3%
Finance	55	14%	254	6%
Real estate & administrative services	37	9%	496	13%
Professional services	57	15%	453	11%
Other services	7	2%	175	4%
Total	391	100%	4006	100%

Source: OECD elaboration based on Sexta Encuesta Longitudinal de Empresas (2019[8]), https://www.ine.cl/estadisticas/economia/ciencia-y-tecnologia/encuesta-longitudinal-de-empresas.

Annex 2.B. Regression results on the effect of foreign ownership on firm performance

Regression analysis is used to examine the impact of foreign ownership on firm performance controlling for sector of activity and firm size. The model is as follow:

$$\log(y_i) = \beta_0 + \beta_1 x_i + \sum_{n=1}^{N} \gamma_n + \sum_{l=1}^{L} \delta_l + \varepsilon_i$$

Where y_i is the performance outcome (e.g. productivity) of firm *i*; x_i is a dummy variable which takes value 1 if firm i is foreign-owned (10% or more of its shares belong to a foreign company) and 0 otherwise; γ are sector-fixed effects (13 sectors), δ captures firm size (5 class sizes) and ε_i is the error term associated to firm i.

Annex Table 2.B.1. Foreign ownership is significantly and positively associated to most performance variables

	log(productivity)	log(export intensity)	log(labour cost per person)	log(share of skilled employees)	log(share of skilled female employees)	log(share of female employees)	log(share of female managers)	log(energy efficiency)
Foreign ownership	0.590***	0.277***	0.533***	0.632***	0.509***	0.0829	-0.158	0.597***
	(0.0788)	(0.0994)	(0.0529)	(0.0751)	(0.0713)	(0.0513)	(0.124)	(0.145)
Firm size	-0.267***	-0.0753***	-0.238***	0.242***	0.295***	0.175***	0.133***	-0.214***
	(0.0175)	(0.00961)	(0.0118)	(0.0198)	(0.025)	(0.0145)	(0.0307)	(0.032)
Constant	7.764***	0.0629**	7.002***	1.912***	3.030***	2.462***	-0.598**	3.794***
	(0.15)	(0.0318)	(0.103)	(0.209)	(0.246)	(0.149)	(0.266)	(0.441)
Observations	3 701	4 397	3 700	2 710	2 127	3 136	265	2 728
R-squared	0.225	0.067	0.309	0.248	0.183	0.244	0.136	0.273
Sector dummies	YES	YES	YES	YES	YES	YES	YES	YES

Note: Sampling weights provided in the Sexta Encuesta Longitudinal de Empresas (ELE6) are used in all regressions. Robust standard errors in parentheses. *** p<0.01, ** p<0.05, * p<0.1.
Source: OECD elaboration based on Sexta Encuesta Longitudinal de Empresas (2019[8]), https://www.ine.cl/estadisticas/economia/ciencia-y-tecnologia/encuesta-longitudinal-de-empresas.

The percentage impact of foreign ownership on y_i can be calculated as 100*[exp*(β1)-1].

Annex Table 2.B.2. Percentage impact of foreign ownership on firm performance

Log(y)	% impact of foreign on Y	Confidence intervals (95%)
productivity	0.80	0.55 – 1.11
labour cost	0.70	0.54 – 0.89
export intensity	0.32	0.09 – 0.60
skill intensity	0.88	0.62 – 1.18

Log(y)	% impact of foreign on Y	Confidence intervals (95%)
skill intensity female employees	0.66	0.46 – 0.91
share of female employees	0.09	-0.02 – 0.20
share of female managers	-0.15	-0.33 – 0.09
energy efficiency	0.82	0.37 – 1.41

Source: OECD elaboration based on Sexta Encuesta Longitudinal de Empresas (2019[8]), https://www.ine.cl/estadisticas/economia/ciencia-y-tecnologia/encuesta-longitudinal-de-empresas.

Annex 2.C. Job creation potential of greenfield FDI

Annex Table 2.C.1. Activities by number of jobs created for 1 million greenfield FDI invested

Sector	Activity	Jobs created per million greenfield FDI
Construction	Hotels & tourism	18.27
	Real estate	13.78
Energy	Renewable energy	0.42
Mining	Metals	1.17
	Coal, oil & gas	0.28
High-tech manufacturing	Consumer electronics	20.34
	Electronic components	12.03
	Pharmaceuticals	4.99
	Business machines & equipment	3.99
	Aerospace	2.94
	Biotechnology	2.34
Medium-tech manufacturing	Consumer products	11
	Automotive components	8.89
	Plastics	6.74
	Minerals	6.10
	Non-automotive transport OEM	5.86
	Engines & turbines	5.09
	Rubber	4.97
	Industrial equipment	4.85
	Automotive OEM	3.9
	Semiconductors	3.89
	Metals	3.33
	Ceramics & glass	3.18
	Chemicals	2.97
	Building materials	2.36
Low-tech manufacturing	Wood products	9.18
	Textiles	5.02
	Food & Beverages	4.44
	Paper, printing & packaging	1.45
Services	Hotels & tourism	13.2
	Software & IT services	8.93
	Healthcare	8.7
	Financial services	2.54
	Business services	2.45
	Real estate	2.02
	Transportation & Warehousing	1.86
	Communications	0.9

Source: OECD elaboration based on fDi Markets (2022[6]), greenfield FDI, https://www.fdimarkets.com/.

Notes

[1] The amount of investments which went to Antofagasta, Atacama and Santiago might be underestimated, since for about 23% of the greenfield projects realised in the period 2010-21, the location is not reported.

[2] Negative FDI positions largely result when the loans from the affiliate to its parent exceed the loans and equity capital given by the parent to the affiliate OECD (2022[42]).

[3] Supplier relationships – when foreign firms purchase inputs from domestic firms – can be a channel for technology and knowledge transfer, for example when foreign firms train suppliers to ensure a certain level of input quality (Javorcik, 2004[40]). Buyer relationships – when foreign firms sell their production as inputs to domestic firms – can help the latter to become more productive mainly through access to better quality inputs (Criscuolo and Timmis, 2017[12]). Many foreign firms in industries such as machinery and the digital economy also offer training to their customers on the use of their products and information on international quality standards (Jindra, 2006[41]).

[4] An earlier version of the report based on the previous version of the survey (ELE5 for 2017) shows slightly different results. According to the indicator based on the ELE5, foreign companies have a productivity premium in all sectors, with the exception of hotels & restaurants and energy. The differences observed between the two surveys are probably related to the different time periods covered and differences in the distribution of companies across sectors. Overall, the results of the two surveys are consistent, as they show that foreign firms are on average more productive in most sectors of the economy. A foreign productivity premium across almost all sectors of the economy is also found using information collected by Chile's Internal Revenue Service. Results are available upon request.

[5] ELE6 does not provide information on R&D activities, so the indicator for R&D activities is constructed using an earlier version of the survey, ELE5 for 2017.

[6] A foreign wage premium is found in most sectors also when using information collected by Chile's Internal Revenue Service. Results are available upon request.

3 Policies to harness FDI for Chile's sustainable development

This chapter assesses the policy and regulatory framework influencing the impact of FDI on sustainable development in Chile, with a focus on productivity, innovation, skills development and the low-carbon transition. Policy recommendations are provided to strengthen the economic, social and environmental benefits of investment and help Chile diversify its production structure towards high-tech and knowledge-intensive economic activities.

3.1. Introduction

Foreign direct investment (FDI) can play a catalytic role in financing the Sustainable Development Goals (SDGs) and supporting inclusive and sustainable recovery and growth (OECD, 2022[1]). As described in Chapter 2, FDI provides technological and financial resources necessary to improve living standards, boost employment, trigger innovation and deliver green growth. However, FDI does not always go where it is most needed and its impacts on sustainable development are not always positive. The quality of the regulatory environment can determine whether a country can attract sustainable investment, and whether spillovers on the domestic economy can occur. A number of more targeted policies at the intersection of investment policy and sustainable development can also avoid negative implications that may result from the presence of foreign firms, such as crowding out of local SMEs, skills and jobs. These laws, regulations and policy initiatives cannot be considered in silos but in the framework of an adequate and coherent policy mix.

Chile's economy boasts sound macroeconomic fundamentals, capitalising on decades of careful economic management as well as political and institutional stability. Over the past ten years, Chile has undertaken ambitious reforms to continue improving its policies, regulations and institutional frameworks in key areas such as environmental sustainability, governance, competition, education, tax policy, and gender equality. An open investment and trade regime and a robust regulatory and institutional environment have supported FDI and made it an important driver of economic growth. Chile is now at a critical junction where many decisions are being taken that are likely to shape the future of its society and economy for years to come. Timely action is needed to harness the potential benefits of FDI as Chile embarks on reforms to strengthen the resilience of the economy and support an inclusive and sustainable recovery in the aftermath of the COVID-19 pandemic.

This chapter reviews the mix of policies in place for strengthening the contribution of FDI to sustainable development in Chile. It provides an overview of policy initiatives implemented by key Ministries and government agencies at the intersection of investment policy and sustainable development, focusing on productivity, innovation, skills development, green growth and the low-carbon transition. It also assesses various aspects of regulation affecting foreign MNEs' sustainable investment decisions, focusing on investment openness, competition policy and labour market regulations, and drawing comparisons with and examples from other OECD economies, which offer significant opportunities for mutual learning. These comparisons are complemented with a set of recommendations on how Chile can use FDI to diversify its production structure and hasten its transition towards a knowledge-based economy.

Policy messages

- Streamline sectoral licensing requirements for high-tech manufacturing and knowledge-intensive services, including by digitalising compliance processes related to setting up a business, acquiring permits and undertaking investments in strategic sectors of the economy. FDI restrictions are limited but approval processes for investment projects (e.g. environmental licenses) are not always clearly defined, sometimes leading to significant delays, uncertainties and discretionary decisions.
- Remove barriers to foreign supplier participation in public procurement and integrate environmental and social criteria into public tenders as well as clearly defined rules to avoid discretionary decisions. Public procurement can be a strategic tool to strengthen the sustainable development impacts of foreign firms and achieve policy goals such as job creation, environmental sustainability and innovation.
- Continue efforts to integrate sustainability considerations into Chile's international trade and investment agreements. Labour and environmental standards are increasingly part of free trade agreements negotiated by the Ministry of Foreign Affairs; however, more could be done to update "old generation" agreements that do not include sustainable development provisions and strengthen their effective implementation.
- Strengthen InvestChile's capacity to target high value-added investments (e.g. through incentives) and measure the contribution of investment promotion activities to the SDGs and sustainability more generally. Sustainability considerations are increasingly part of InvestChile's investment promotion activities, including through the prioritisation of low-carbon, technology-intensive and high value added FDI projects. Further efforts in this area could involve broadening the scope of indicators used by the agency for monitoring and evaluating its activities.
- Consider ways to strengthen InvestChile's investment promotion activities in key markets abroad, including by establishing overseas offices and strengthening co-ordination with ProChile and the Ministry of Foreign Affairs. Currently, InvestChile collaborates with ProChile's international network of offices to promote Chile as an attractive investment destination abroad, but joint activities are limited and take place on an ad hoc basis.
- Specify policy co-ordination mechanisms and monitoring and evaluation (M&E) tools for the implementation of the National Strategy for the Promotion of Foreign Investment. The strategy lacks a comprehensive description of the institutions that should be involved and of the governance arrangements that are needed to achieve the investment policy objectives set.
- Adjust the R&D tax incentive scheme to make it more attractive for foreign and domestic firms that seek to engage in innovation-based partnerships. Reporting and other compliance constraints limit the scheme's overall effectiveness in incentivising R&D-intensive investment. Consider the role that InvestChile's aftercare services could play in encouraging established investors to undertake R&D activities in Chile.
- Consider ways to streamline and consolidate Chile's investment incentives framework to support the financing of low-carbon and technology-intensive investments, including through enhanced co-ordination and joint management of the incentives system or through new funding tools by CORFO and the Banco del Estado. Although financial support for productive investments is offered by several public institutions, Chile provides one of the lowest levels of total government support for business R&D and innovation among OECD and partner economies.

- Implement FDI-SME linkage programmes and provide technical assistance to domestic firms, in particular SMEs, to help them become successful suppliers and partners of foreign investors. Knowledge spillovers from FDI will not materialise unless domestic firms' capacities are aligned with the needs of investors. To this end, joint policy initiatives could be undertaken by InvestChile, CORFO and Sercotec.
- Incentivise foreign MNEs to undertake training activities for their employees and local suppliers, by encouraging greater levels of permanent employment and allowing firms to tailor skills development programmes to the needs of their employees. Better co-ordination between InvestChile, CORFO and SENCE will be key to improve FDI's contribution to skills development.
- Continue policy efforts to create an enabling environment for renewable energy investments by removing regulatory barriers, providing specific incentives, and reforming the current carbon pricing framework. Chile's long-term goal of at least 80% renewable energy by 2050 will require policy co-ordination and consultation with industry to keep a fast pace of investment in clean energy.
- Explore measures to attract investment in the emerging green hydrogen industry – while taking into consideration the early technological maturity of hydrogen technologies and the high risks involved – including through public-private partnerships, incentives for investments in enabling infrastructure, capacity building and training programmes, R&D collaborations and regulation addressing demand-side bottlenecks.

3.2. The regulatory framework for investment

3.2.1. Chile's economy is open to FDI, but challenges remain for foreign firms

The type of FDI that a country attracts and the extent to which foreign firms can contribute to sustainable development depend, among other factors, on the regulatory environment for FDI and the legal framework for market entry and conduct. Openness to FDI may not only affect productivity and competitiveness in industries that get market access, but also those in downstream sectors that benefit from potentially better access to high quality inputs and services domestically.

The sound macroeconomic fundamentals, judicial security as well as economic and political stability of the past decades have made Chile one of the strongest investment destinations in the LAC region. Chile's statutory restrictions to foreign investment are slightly below the OECD average according to the OECD FDI Regulatory Restrictiveness (FDIRR) index, which gauges the restrictiveness of a country's FDI rules (Figure 3.1). The Chilean regulatory framework for FDI is also less restrictive than non-OECD LAC countries such as Peru, Brazil and Argentina. Investment-related regulations are non-discriminatory and foreign-owned enterprises are provided with national treatment, i.e. they have the right to establish a business enterprise under the same terms and conditions as domestic firms.

At the sectoral level, certain market access restrictions are found in transport and fisheries (Figure 3.2). For instance, foreign ownership in the maritime freight sector is capped while international reciprocity restrictions are in place for fisheries. In the media and broadcasting sectors, there are no foreign equity restrictions, but some limitations apply. There is a reciprocity requirement for the granting and use of radio broadcasting concessions, and key personnel of broadcasting companies must be Chilean citizens. Beyond these sectoral limitations, foreign investors must obtain specific authorisation to invest in strategic sectors such as the exploration and exploitation of hydrocarbons, mining or the production of nuclear energy. The Chilean Constitution stipulates the exclusive control of the State over all mineral, hydrocarbon and fossil fuel deposits, but the government is allowed to grant concession rights to foreign and domestic companies for exploration and exploitation activities.

Figure 3.1. Chile's statutory restrictions to foreign investment are close to the OECD average

OECD FDI Regulatory Restrictiveness Index, 2020 (open=0; closed=1)

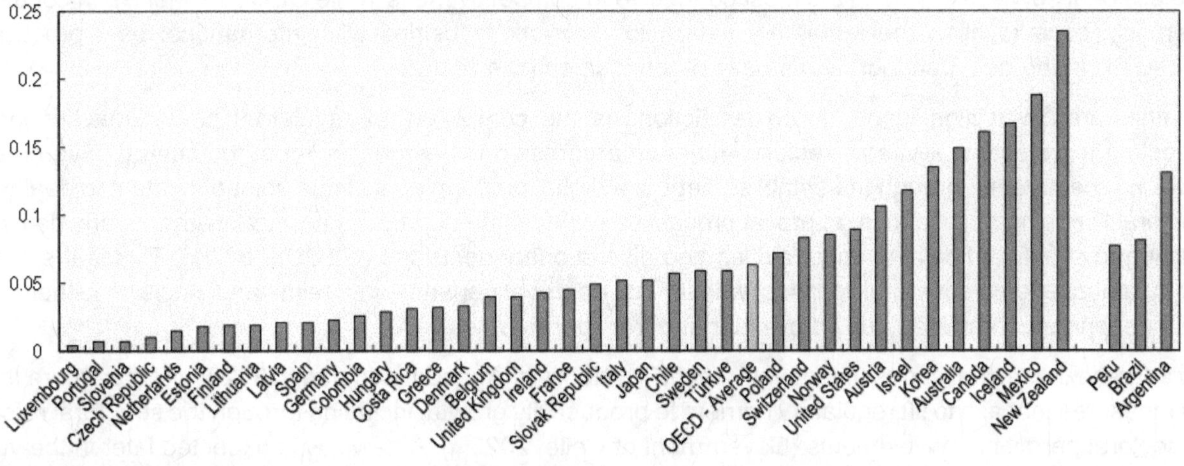

Note: The OECD FDI Regulatory Restrictiveness Index only covers statutory measures discriminating against foreign investors.
Source: OECD FDI Regulatory Restrictiveness Index (2020[2]), www.oecd.org/investment/fdiindex.htm

Figure 3.2. FDI restrictions are limited to a handful of sectors

OECD FDI Regulatory Restrictiveness Index, overall and sector-specific, 2020

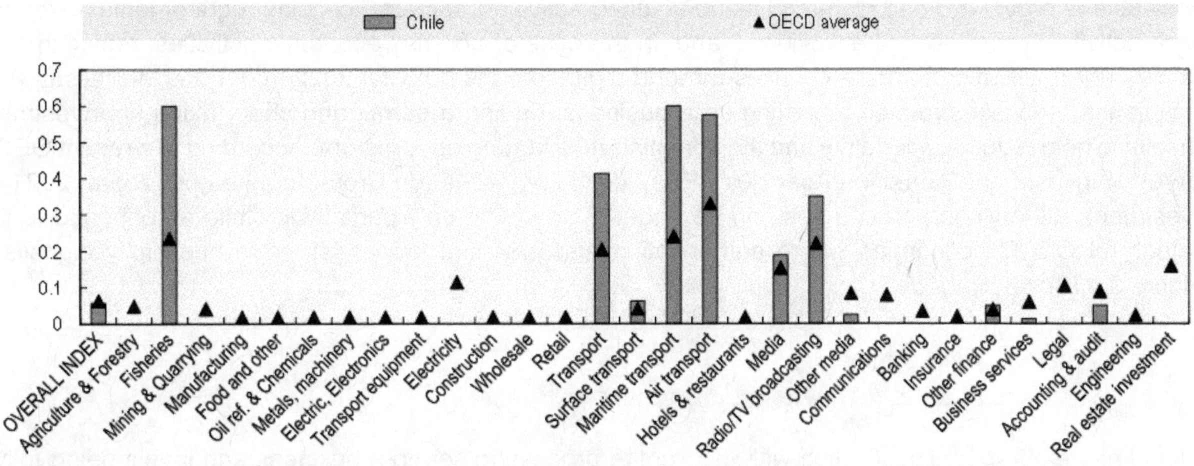

Source: OECD FDI Regulatory Restrictiveness Index (2020[2]), www.oecd.org/investment/fdiindex.htm

The literature suggests that in many OECD economies, beyond FDI restrictions, there are also 'behind-the-border' regulations, including restrictions in trade, barriers to competition and other discriminatory measures that influence market access conditions not only in industries where FDI gains access but also in downstream sectors from which foreign firms can source their inputs and create supply chain linkages with domestic enterprises. Pro-competitive measures can support productivity growth by incentivising existing firms to innovate and adopt better technologies while also supporting the reallocation of resources towards more productive firms.

Overall, regulatory barriers to competition in Chile are very close to the OECD average (Figure 3.3, Panel A). The presence of the state in the economy through the ownership of firms is limited when compared with most other OECD countries, in particular regarding ownership of shares in the largest operators in network sectors. The administrative burden on business and regulatory barriers in service sectors are below those present in many OECD countries. Similarly, regulation of retail trade and professional services is among the most conducive to competitiveness in the OECD (Panel B). In contrast, there is scope to align the regulatory set-up for network industries with international best practices, especially in the gas, transport and mobile e-communications sectors.

Another area with significantly more restrictions is the complexity of regulatory procedures for large investment projects in strategic sectors. Although progress has been achieved at the central government level in recent years through the establishment of a digital platform as a single point of contact to deal with sectoral licensing applications; approval processes for investment projects are not always clearly defined, leading to significant delays, uncertainties and discretionary decisions (OECD, 2022[3]). This is the case, for instance, of environmental licenses, whose final approval depends on a ministerial decision rather than an independent committee guided by clear and transparent rules.

To address these challenges, the government's Productivity Agenda, adopted in 2023, includes more than 40 measures that aim to lift regulatory barriers to productivity growth, including through the structural reform of sectoral permits for investments (Government of Chile, 2023[4]). A new law is expected later in the year to streamline administrative processes for five key permits for which excessive delays are usually observed (e.g. maritime concessions, construction permits, licensing for hydraulic works and excavations), and strengthen co-ordination between the relevant authorities. These reforms are a step in the right direction since they could significantly reduce the complexity of certain administrative procedures and facilitate the granting of construction permits.

As Chile seeks to diversify the type of FDI that it attracts away from natural resources and towards renewable energy, R&D and high-tech manufacturing activities, sectoral licensing requirements governing these activities could be further reviewed and, in the case of non-risk economic activities, replaced by a simple prior notification to the authorities through digital means (OECD, 2022[3]). Further digitalisation of compliance processes related to setting up a business, getting a permit and undertaking an investment could also help reduce uncertainty and the administrative burden on investors. According to a recent OECD survey of Investment Promotion Agencies (IPAs)' digital practices (de Crombrugghe and Moore, 2021[5]), investment authorisation procedures can be undertaken online only partially in Chile as opposed to the majority of OECD economies where authorisation and payment processes have been fully digitalised (Figure 3.4, Box 3.1).

Box 3.1. Digitalisation of the investment process in Israel

Israel has embraced digitalisation with their entire process to set up a business and invest being fully online, including the procedures related to the investment authorisation and required payments. Invest in Israel's website provides a short questionnaire that makes an investing manual specific to the needs of the investor according to the company profile. The online tailored investment manual provides the necessary information on registering the company, land tenure, building permits, business licensing, operations as well as information on grants and benefits. The manual details the necessary steps and documents as well as the costs and time frame for each aspect of the investment process.

Source: De Crombrugghe and Moore (2021[5]), www.oecd.org/daf/inv/investment-policy/Investment-Insights-Investment-Promotion-Digital-Economy-OECD.pdf

Figure 3.3. Pro-competitive regulation compares well on average, but challenges remain for foreign firms

OECD Product Market Regulation, 2018 (most competitive=0; least competitive=6)

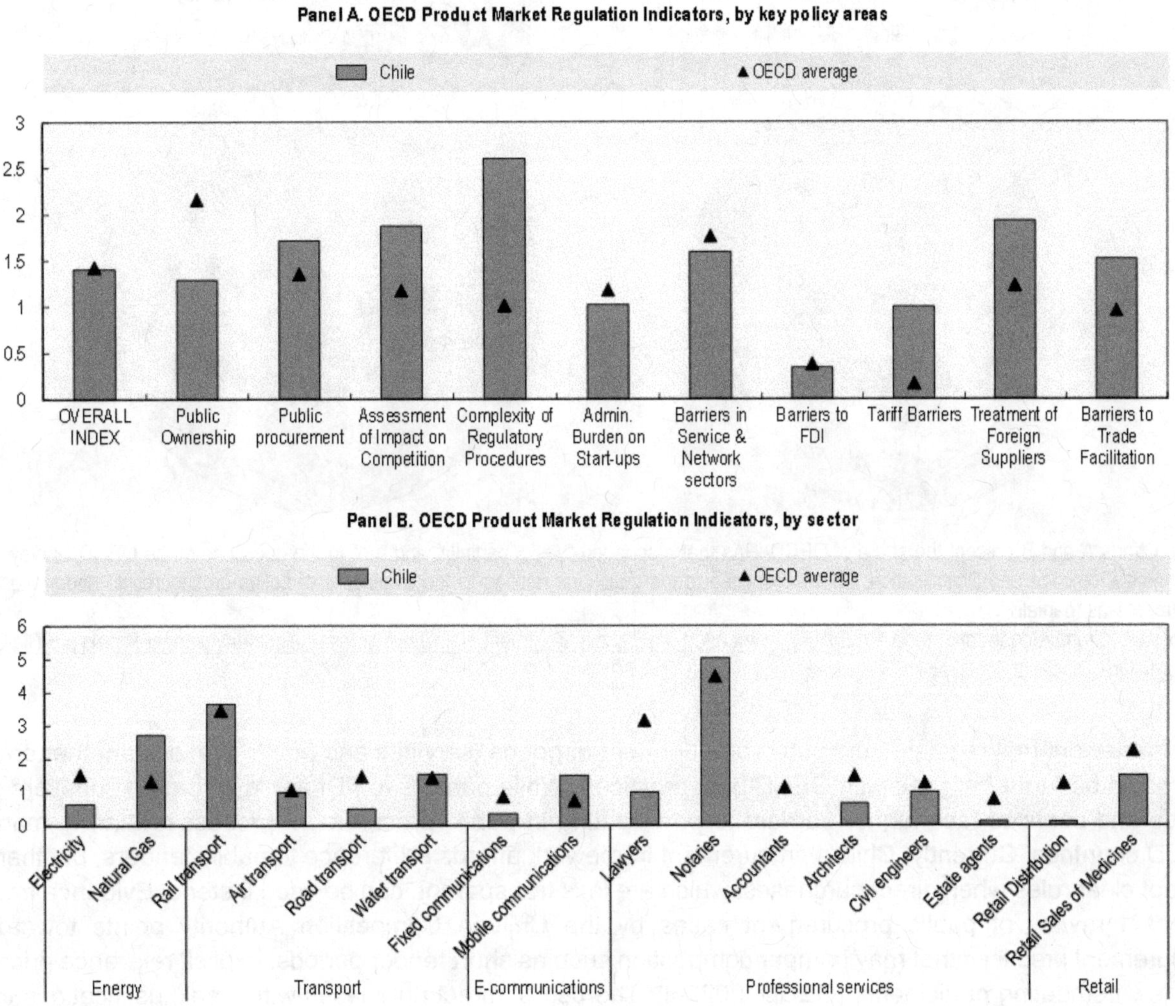

Note: Index scale 0 to 6 from most to least pro-competitive regulation.
Source: OECD Indicators of Product Market Regulation, (2018[6]), www.oecd.org/economy/reform/indicators-of-product-market-regulation/

Figure 3.4. Availability of online procedures to undertake an investment in Chile and all other OECD countries

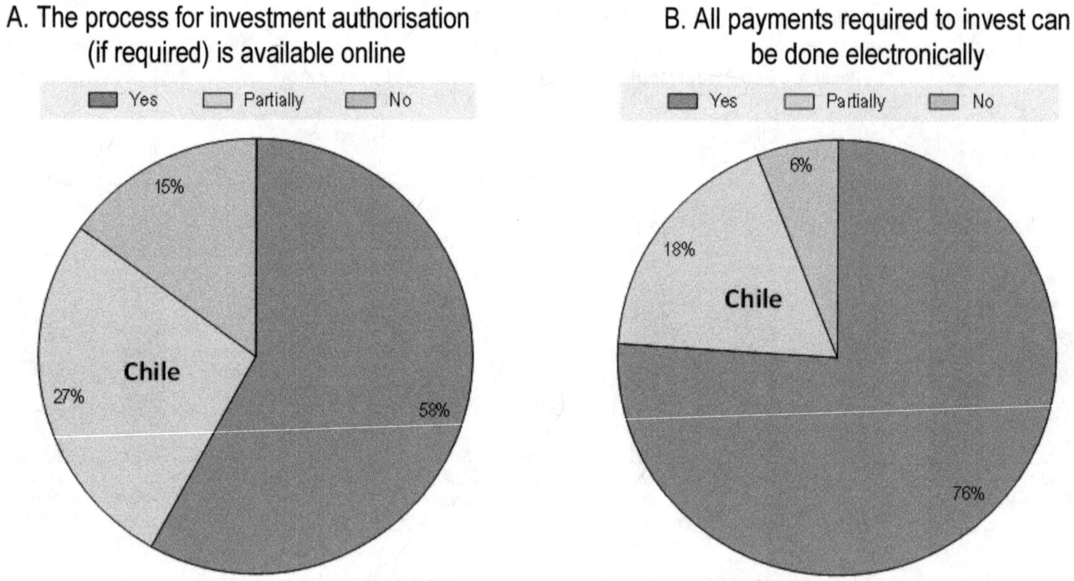

Notes: Charts A and B present the share of OECD IPAs that responded "yes", "partially" and "no" to the questions of the OECD Survey on Investment Promotion and Digitalisation. Chile's response to the questions relating to the availability of online procedures to undertake an investment was "partially".
Source: de Crombrugghe and Moore (2021[5]), www.oecd.org/daf/inv/investment-policy/Investment-Insights-Investment-Promotion-Digital-Economy-OECD.pdf

The framework that regulates the public procurement of goods, services and public works is another area that could be further aligned with OECD best practices. While barriers to FDI are low, foreign suppliers of goods and services face higher barriers to participating in public procurement processes than in many OECD countries. Currently, Chile's procurement framework affords preference to public tenders, but there are not clear rules when direct purchases, which are less transparent, can be used instead. Evidence from a recent review of public procurement cases by the Chilean Competition Authority points towards procurement practices that may hamper competition such as short tender periods, explicit reference prices and few competing participants (OECD, 2022[3]). The use of direct purchases with weak justifications for sidestepping public tenders appears to also be widespread in the public administration.

The Chilean Government could consider the role of public procurement as a strategic tool for strengthening the sustainable development impacts of foreign multinational enterprises (MNEs). In addition to improving efficiency and value for money, public procurement involves significant funds and is used to deliver public services to citizens as well as to achieve policy goals such as job creation, the development of small and medium enterprises (SMEs), environmental sustainability or innovation. The buying power of governments can be a lever for promoting sustainable investment practices, in particular in sectors of strategic importance for the Chilean economy. Removing barriers to foreign supplier participation should be combined with the integration of environmental and social criteria in public procurement tenders as well as clearly defined rules to avoid discretionary decisions and ensure their integrity and accountability.

Such a public procurement framework could be a useful tool to decarbonise infrastructure investment. If used in combination with long-term power purchasing agreements (PPAs), tenders can be an alternative way to attract private investment in clean energy. In Brazil, for example, the use of reverse auctions for wind energy (with 20-year PPAs) resulted in winning bids for which tariff rates were 42% lower than previously established feed-in-tariffs (OECD, 2022[1]). Integrating environmental criteria into tenders will, however, require technical capacity in the renewable energy field from procuring authorities. Co-ordination with sectoral ministries will be key for the successful implementation and outcome of tenders. Simplified procurement procedures, including through electronic systems, may also help ease the process and increase competition, including further involvement of foreign MNEs.

3.2.2. Sustainability considerations could be further mainstreamed into Chile's international trade and investment agreements

International trade and investment agreements that are aligned with climate objectives, international labour standards and principles on gender equality and encourage co-operation and monitoring of commitments can complement government efforts to enhance the positive impact of investment on sustainable development (OECD, 2022[1]). Provisions in these international agreements can be designed to allow treaty parties to make commitments to strengthen domestic law regulation and enforcement in several key areas relating to the qualities of FDI.

Chile is one of the leading Latin American countries in trade and investment treaty-making. In previous decades, Chile engaged in the negotiation of a wide-ranging network of bilateral investment treaties and preferential trade agreements that led to low tariffs and higher trade and investment, GDP per capita and employment (OECD, 2018[7]). The Ministry of Foreign Affairs' Undersecretariat for International Economic Relations (SUBREI) is responsible for negotiating international treaties on economic, trade and investment policy matters. It also supervises Chile's network of diplomatic missions abroad, including commercial offices, in collaboration with ProChile, the country's export promotion agency.

Chile's general investment treaty policy has been to negotiate investment chapters in Free Trade Agreements (FTAs). In this context, the number of bilateral investment treaties (BITs) concluded over the past two decades has decreased considerably. Since 2010 Chile has negotiated only two international investment agreements (IIAs) with Uruguay (in 2010) and Hong Kong (in 2016) that establish commitments to liberalise and protect foreign investment (SUBREI, 2022[8]). They both include a dedicated article recognising the parties' right to take any measure to ensure that investment activities consider environmental and public health objectives. However, they fall short of making specific references to international labour standards, gender provisions, the OECD Guidelines for Multinational Enterprises, and the right to regulate.

Chile has concluded 11 FTAs with investment chapters that establish liberalisation commitments as well as protection standards for said investments (SUBREI, 2022[8]). As opposed to older FTAs, more recent agreements (e.g. FTAs with Canada, Brazil and Pacific Alliance countries) have been significantly geared towards sustainable development principles (e.g. gender, labour and responsible business conduct standards) (Table 3.1). For instance, Chile's FTA with Brazil entered into force in 2022 and includes dedicated chapters on SMEs, labour standards, the environment, and gender equality. The agreement's investment chapter also contains explicit provisions acknowledging that investors should contribute to social and environmental objectives, respect human rights, promote human capital development, build trust with local communities, and strengthen domestic productive capacities, amongst other objectives.

Similar language is found in FTAs that have been recently updated following renewed bilateral negotiations to reflect new areas of interest for the parties involved. The amended FTA with Canada came into force in 2019 with updated language that reaffirms the state's right to regulate in the public interest and a new dedicated article on corporate social responsibility (Government of Canada, 2019[9]). A new chapter on trade and gender was also included acknowledging the importance of applying a gender perspective to economic issues to ensure that the benefits of trade and investment are realised in all parts of society.

The inclusion of such provisions in recent agreements is a step in the right direction. The relevance of these provisions will depend on their implementation, however. The bulk of Chile's IIAs, most of which were concluded in previous decades, does not contain strong commitments to sustainable development principles, and when they do, references are mainly found in the preamble of FTAs (WTI, 2022[10]). Chile could continue efforts to integrate sustainability considerations into new IIAs while at the same time engage in dialogue with its international partners to explore opportunities to update "old generation" agreements (as was the case with Canada). Efforts should be also made to improve the quality of these provisions by ensuring that they make reference to a wider set of sustainability principles and international standards (e.g. ILO and RBC standards), and are not limited to the preamble of IIAs but are rather entrenched into the text of the treaties.

Table 3.1. Sustainable development provisions in investment chapters of Free Trade Agreements signed by Chile

	Sustainable development provisions
US – Chile Free Trade Agreement	Article 10.12 – Investment and Environment: "Nothing in this chapter shall be construed to prevent a Party from adopting, maintaining, or enforcing any measure otherwise consistent with this chapter that it considers appropriate to ensure that investment activity in its territory is undertaken in a manner sensitive to environmental concerns".
Chile – Canada Free Trade Agreement	Article G-14: Environmental Measures: "The Parties recognise that it is inappropriate to encourage investment by relaxing domestic health, safety or environmental measures. Accordingly, a Party should not waive or otherwise derogate from, or offer to waive or otherwise derogate from, such measures as an encouragement for the establishment, acquisition, expansion or retention in its territory of an investment of an investor."
	Article G-14 bis: Corporate Social Responsibility: "The Parties reaffirm their commitment to internationally recognised standards, guidelines and principles of corporate social responsibility that have been endorsed or are supported by the Parties, including the OECD Guidelines for Multinational Enterprises, and each Party should encourage enterprises operating within its territory or subject to its jurisdiction to voluntarily incorporate these standards, guidelines and principles into their business practices and internal policies."
Chile – Brazil Free Trade Agreement	Article 8.15 –Social Responsibility Policies: "Investors and their investments should develop their best efforts to comply with the OECD Guidelines for Multinational Enterprises of the Organization for Economic Co-operation and Development, in particular: (a) Contribute to economic, social and environmental progress, with a view to achieving sustainable development; (b) Respect the internationally recognised human rights of people involved in the activities of the companies; (c) Stimulate the generation of local capacities through close collaboration with the local community; (d) Promote the formation of human capital, especially through the creation of employment opportunities, and offering training to employees; (e) Refrain from seeking or accepting exemptions not contemplated in the legal framework or regulatory framework related to human rights, the environment, health, security, work, tax system, financial incentives, or other questions."

Source: OECD elaboration based on SUBREI (2022[11]), www.subrei.gob.cl/acuerdos-comerciales/acuerdos-comerciales-vigentes

3.3. Leveraging investment promotion and facilitation for Chile's sustainable development

3.3.1. InvestChile could further improve its capacity to track and measure the contribution of investment promotion activities to the SDGs

IPAs are key players in bridging information gaps that may otherwise hinder the realisation of foreign investments, and their potential sustainable development impacts. Most IPAs prioritise certain types of investments over others, by selecting priority sectors, countries or investment projects, and allocating resources accordingly. InvestChile's organisational structures and strategies, just like that of other IPAs worldwide, have evolved over time, with increased focus on technological change and sustainable development. Since its creation in 2016, the core roles and responsibilities of the agency are to promote inward FDI and support the economic development of national and subnational regions (OECD, 2015[12]). Central to its mission is the provision of business consulting, information and facilitation services that promote high value-added investment and contribute to the diversification of the Chilean economy.

Based on the number and type of responsibilities, InvestChile can be categorised as a specialised type of agency, focusing on investment attraction and investment-related mandates, as is the case for the Czech or Irish agencies, for example. Other IPAs around the world have included additional responsibilities such as innovation and export facilitation. The number and type of mandates can affect the level of resources that IPAs devote to each task and the degree of co-ordination with complementary policies, particularly those related to sustainable development priorities. InvestChile's narrow mandate does not necessarily undermine its capacity to promote investment that brings social and environmental benefits, but it does mean that robust policy co-ordination mechanisms are necessary to maximise synergies with other parts of the government that operate at the intersection of investment promotion and sustainable development. It also means that sustainability considerations in relation to investment promotion should be further mainstreamed into the agency's core functions and activities.

This has been reflected in the evolving focus of InvestChile's sector- and country-based targeting strategy. In recent years, InvestChile has developed new initiatives to improve the quality of its investment promotion activities and pro-actively target foreign MNEs that contribute to FDI diversification. Notable examples are the *Invest in Chile Now* initiative, which began during the COVID-19 crisis and aimed to proactively seek out leading businesses that have the potential to undertake high value-added investment projects. The campaign was carried out primarily through business intelligence, bilateral meetings and tailor-made value propositions addressed to MNEs operating in strategic markets around the world. Over 2020-22, several promotional activities were undertaken in the Middle East and Asia regions, and emphasis was placed on promoting investments in the renewable energy, finance, infrastructure, technological services and agribusiness industries. The prioritisation of low-carbon, technology-intensive and high value added FDI is reflected in InvestChile's portfolio of clients. In 2021, 42% of the supported FDI projects took place in knowledge-intensive services and the technology industry, followed by the agri-food (18%) and energy (11%) sectors (Figure 3.5, Panel A). In terms of value, almost half of supported investments went into the renewables energy sector followed by tourism and mining (Panel B).

Figure 3.5. InvestChile prioritises investments in energy and technology-intensive services, 2021

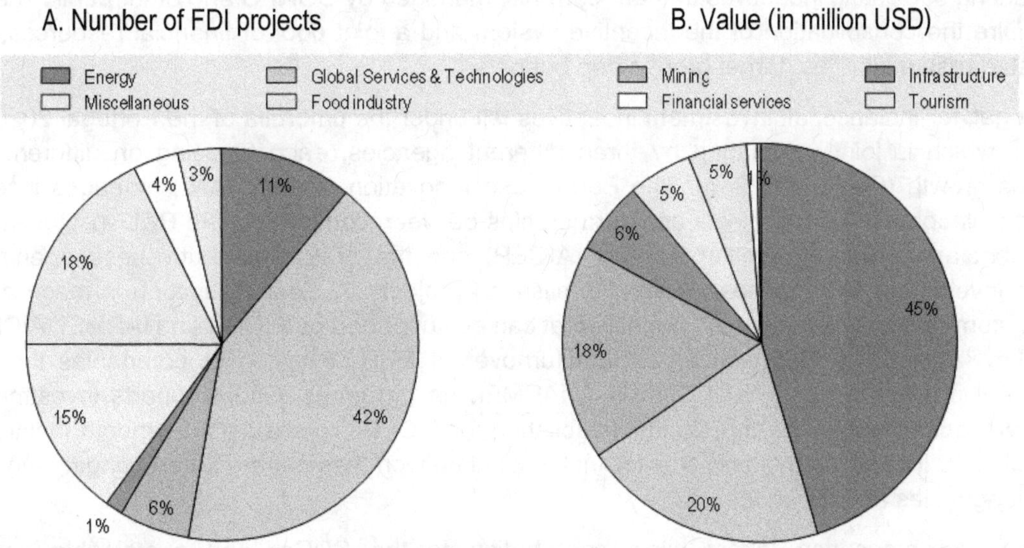

Source: OECD elaboration based on InvestChile (2022[13]), https://investchile.gob.cl/wp-content/uploads/2022/03/reporte-ied-en-chile-a-marzo2022.pdf

As part of its aftercare services, the agency has supported better measurement of sustainability-related outcomes of foreign MNEs. For instance, the *"Measure what matters"* programme, implemented since 2020, seeks to promote the adoption of sustainable investment practices among foreign MNEs that have already set up their operations in Chile and are part of the agency's client portfolio. The programme is free of charge, lasts four months and involves an evaluation of the economic, social and environmental performance of companies and their contribution to the 2010 Agenda for Sustainable Development. Emphasis has been also placed on strengthening collaboration with subnational governments, many of which have developed specialised programmes, units and services with the support of InvestChile to promote foreign investment in their regions. InvestChile is currently implementing a Regional Plan to attract investments according to the development objectives of each region, including through a diagnosis of local investment opportunities and gaps, training of subnational government officials on investment promotion, development of regional value offers and pilot initiatives to improve regional capacities.

Although these initiatives strengthen the role of sustainability in investment promotion, due consideration should be given to the scope and complementarity of policies implemented by InvestChile. While the agency is the first point of contact for many foreign investors and the main government body providing information and technical assistance to foreign firms, it does not have the mandate to provide incentives to stimulate particular types of investment. Incentives are instead provided by the Chilean Economic Development Agency (CORFO) and other public agencies (see Section 3.4.2 and Table 3.2). Effective targeting requires a mix of different types of policy instruments that support firms at every stage of the investment process. In the early 2000s, the Government of Chile had successfully implemented the High Technology Investment Promotion Programme, which is a good example of how a more diverse range of policy instruments combining financial support, technical assistance and greater co-ordination among the various agencies can promote investments of high technological intensity (Box 3.2). A similar programme could be implemented by InvestChile, in collaboration with other public agencies, to complement existing promotional initiatives in emerging industries such as renewables (e.g. green hydrogen industry), ICTs and high-technology manufacturing.

Furthermore, the government could consider how investment promotion activities and incentive schemes could be better integrated and streamlined to create a continuum of support to foreign firms. One option would be for InvestChile to acquire its own financial incentives that could freely use for its clients. An alternative, potentially complementary, option would be for InvestChile to be involved in the administration and granting of existing incentives that are currently managed by CORFO and other public agencies. This will require the consolidation of the incentive system and a joint pool of financial resources, but clearly delineated responsibilities, target groups and budgets.

In Portugal, for instance, all investment incentives fall under the umbrella of the Portugal 2020 Incentives System, which is jointly managed by three different agencies, each focusing on different aspects of business growth (OECD, 2022[14]). The Portuguese Innovation Agency (ANI) manages incentives that support collaborative R&D projects and partnerships between companies and R&D institutions, while the Investment and Trade Promotion Agency (AICEP) and the SME Competitiveness Agency (IAPMEI) support investment and business internationalisation projects. A clear distinction is made between the types of companies and investment projects that can be supported by AICEP and IAPMEI. AICEP's clients are solely large companies with an annual turnover of EUR 75 million or companies that implement investment projects of over EUR 25 million. IAPMEI, on the other hand, supports investment projects whose value is less than the thresholds established for AICEP. To ensure the smooth functioning of the Portugal 2020 Incentives System, an inter-institutional network has been created bringing together all the relevant agencies and ministries.

Tracking and measuring InvestChile's contribution to the SDGs, and sustainable and inclusive development in general, could be also improved further. Currently, InvestChile tracks a set of basic key performance indicators (KPIs), relating mostly to productivity and job creation, such as total value of investment and number of jobs. These indicators are common among OECD IPAs: 90% of them use productivity and innovation performance indicators, and 87% use indicators linked to job creation and skills. However, over time OECD IPAs have added additional and more targeted criteria, including those related to sustainability and inclusiveness, to their KPI toolkit. For example, about half use low-carbon transition-related indicators and one-third of them KPIs on digital transformation (Sztajerowska and Volpe Martincus, 2021[15]). In addition, many IPAs include metrics related to the quality of jobs created (e.g. average wage, occupational characteristics). Finally, numerous OECD IPAs developed dedicated sustainability scoring mechanisms (SSM), i.e. sets of predefined sustainability-related criteria beyond the sheer sector of operation of the investor, to guide their prioritisation efforts. Over 40% of OECD IPAs had such a mechanism in place by September 2022 (at the time of OECD survey on the subject) and several other agencies are working on its implementation.

In the future, the set of indicators and approaches used by InvestChile for M&E could be expanded to consider a broader set of sustainability-related considerations and obtain finer insights on activities of foreign firms in the economy. It could be considered which specific indicators could be usefully added, given the overall policy objectives, the type of data available, among others. The OECD stands ready to support the agency in this reflection and the analysis of specific best practices in this area. For instance, cross-checking data provided by investors with the official statistics and tracking a wider range of firm-level data through the agency's customer relationship management (CRM) system could help evaluate the impact of investment promotion activities in a more consistent and accurate way. In some countries, IPAs are also able to gain access to administrative data on firm-level emissions, energy consumption and other environmental and social variables from environmental protection, certification and emission-disclosure monitoring bodies. In the case of Chile, the national Register of Emissions and Transfers of Pollutants includes such data for both industrial and non-industrial activities. If combined with the internal data available to InvestChile on their assistance to foreign MNEs, it could provide valuable insights into the potential climate contribution of assisted and non-assisted investment projects.

Box 3.2. CORFO's High-technology Investment Promotion Programme

In the early 2000s, CORFO implemented the High-Technology Investment Promotion Programme, which aimed to attract high-tech investments that could diversify Chile's productive base and position the country as an export platform of technological services in the Latin America region (Agosin, 2009[16]). The programme included financial incentives, coupled with technical assistance and information provision, for the adoption of advanced technologies, the implementation of employee training programmes, and the completion of pre-feasibility studies; promotional campaigns and targeted investment generation activities in major tech hubs around the world; and network development initiatives to transfer international best practices from American and European markets to Chile.

The programme's design was based on the experience of other countries, in particular Ireland and Costa Rica, whose investment promotion approach involved the targeting of incentives to specific sectors, emphasis on the technological content of promoted investments, and the use of direct subsidies rather than tax exemptions. In Chile, the prioritisation of high-technology sectors was done in line with the strategic objectives identified by the National Innovation Council for Competitiveness, an inter-institutional body responsible for co-ordinating and advising the government on innovation, science and technology policy (Agosin, 2009[16]). Efforts focused on attracting firms that could contribute to the development of the clusters identified by the Council as having the greatest potential for economic growth such as ICTs, biotechnologies and new materials.

Although the programme's budget and number of staff were small by international standards, CORFO managed to leverage the expertise of various government actors and international stakeholders. A team of government agencies was created to facilitate investment promotion activities, bringing together the National Commission for Science and Technology, Fundación Chile, a non-profit foundation that supported new technological applications in a number of industries, and Chile's official IPA, the Foreign Investment Committee (Nelson, 2007[17]). To ensure alignment of the programme with industry priorities,

CORFO also created a transnational strategic network consisting of a business school in the United States, sectoral experts associated with successful IPAs, US-based consulting firms specialising in business services, software development and ICTs, US business associations and foreign investors established in Chile. All played an important role in the effective development and evolution of the programme.

In 2001-03, 219 companies had received technical assistance, including information and advice for the evaluation of investment opportunities and conditions in Chile. Overall, for each US dollar of public financial support provided to foreign investors, the programme had yielded USD 10 of materialised investments (Agosin, 2009[16]). Thanks to the programme, in 2007, there were 60 international technology service centres operating in the country and leading companies in the ICT, business services, and software development sectors had been established in Chile.

Source: OECD based on Agosin (2009[16]) and Nelson (2007[17]).

3.3.2. Overseas offices and stronger collaboration between InvestChile and ProChile could help target investors in strategic markets abroad

InvestChile's collaboration with the Ministry of Foreign Affairs and ProChile, the country's export promotion agency, could be leveraged to promote Chile as an attractive investment destination in key markets abroad, reach out to potential investors and generate leads and investment projects that contribute to sustainable development. Co-ordination with diplomatic missions in foreign countries can be very important for IPAs and for investment promotion in general because it spearheads the efforts of a country to promote itself and establish strategic relationships with investor networks abroad (OECD, 2018[18]). These relationships can also foster strong ties with economic diplomacy, including foreign trade policy, and help attract export-oriented investors that will set up their business activities in Chile to trade with the LAC region and the rest of the world.

Currently, InvestChile's presence abroad includes six representatives. Three representatives report directly to InvestChile and serve as regional contact points for Asia, Europe and North America, while the other three are presidential attachés, appointed by the President, but co-ordinated by InvestChile, assigned to Rome, Ottawa and Paris. In addition, there is ad hoc collaboration with the Undersecretariat for International Economic Relations (SUBREI) of the Ministry of Foreign Affairs and ProChile's international network of offices. The latter includes 57 international commercial offices, which primarily aim to connect Chilean exporters with companies abroad and provide them with tailored information on how to access foreign markets. Although ProChile's offices have been given a formal mandate to work on investment promotion in co-ordination with InvestChile and SUBREI, in practice joint investment promotion activities are limited and take place on an ad hoc basis. Lack of resources, overlaps between investment promotion and other foreign policy mandates and absence of clearly defined roles and responsibilities are the major factors making co-ordination complex and ineffective.

InvestChile could consider establishing a small number of own overseas offices abroad in the form of "regional hubs" which will cover specific continental regions and be tasked with image building and investment generation activities in collaboration with Chile's diplomatic missions and ProChile's offices (e.g. organising sector- or investor-specific missions abroad, handling investor enquiries and requests, implementing pro-active campaigns). These satellite offices would be better positioned to lead investment promotion activities in strategic markets, ensure consistency in the country brand messaging and information delivered to potential investors, and foster greater synergies with Chile's existing network of agencies and representations abroad. IDA Ireland, for example, shares local market plans and teams with embassies abroad (OECD, 2018[18]). Invest in Canada, in addition to its network of 35 offices abroad, relies on some 140 diplomatic missions around the world. Among them, 24 are located in strategic markets and are tasked to actively attract FDI, whereas other missions are given "reactive" mandates.

Existing mechanisms for co-ordination with ProChile and the Ministry of Foreign Affairs should be also strengthened to foster economies of scale in countries in which InvestChile will not be present but still offer opportunities for investment generation. Such collaboration will need well-functioning processes and mechanisms such as shared customer relationship management systems, dedicated communication channels and tools, and clear and well-defined responsibilities to enable follow-up on investment project leads and requests. These strategic links could be formalised through inter-agency collaboration agreements (e.g. contracts, MoUs) that define the responsibilities of each institution and specify the internal management processes that will be used for the delivery of investment promotion services.

3.3.3. The new National Strategy for FDI Promotion will require robust inter-institutional co-ordination mechanisms for its successful implementation

In 2022, Chile's Inter-ministerial Committee for the Promotion of Foreign Investment adopted a new national strategy on FDI promotion, which places foreign investment at the epicentre of Chile's economic transformation agenda. The strategy identifies the low degree of FDI diversification, high concentration in natural resources and limited FDI flows into manufacturing (discussed in Chapter 2) as key challenges for the Chilean economy. It also explicitly reflects Chile's emerging policy priorities relating to FDI diversification and sustainable development by proposing to build the country's strategic framework for investment promotion around four key themes, namely FDI growth, economic transformation, sustainability and impact.

The strategy revises InvestChile's investment prioritisation framework, which has so far focused on the targeting of a limited number of sectors, and suggests instead a flexible approach that relies on 17 criteria linking investment projects to specific activities and performance outcomes. For instance, the agency has been tasked with targeting investment projects that are aligned with the SDGs and responsible business conduct (RBC) standards; contribute to addressing global challenges such as digital transformation, the climate crisis and technological disruption; foster business linkages with local supplier ecosystems; and support the development of highly skilled human capital, quality jobs and technology transfers to the local economy, amongst others. The implementation of this new framework will rely on several action plans that will be developed and executed annually by InvestChile and the various ministries that make up the inter-ministerial committee. The plans will include specific actions, establish objectives and identify target markets and performance criteria that investment projects should fulfil. A novelty of the action plans is that their objectives and actions will be also linked to concrete proposals for policy initiatives and government reforms to address potential regulatory barriers or underdeveloped capacities in the Chilean economy. This is expected to strengthen InvestChile's policy advocacy role by monitoring foreign investors' perception of the country's investment climate and proposing changes to improve investment policy.

Although the strategy includes several references to the need for inter-institutional co-ordination to successfully implement the new investment policy priorities, it lacks a comprehensive description of the institutions that should be involved and of the governance arrangements that are needed to achieve the objectives set by the inter-ministerial committee. As Chile has entered a new policy cycle and sustainability considerations are already increasingly mainstreamed into investment policy, the lack of clarity around the strategy's governance model increases the risk of policy overlaps and contradictions and could lead to ambiguity about the pursued policy objectives and the responsibilities of various institutions. In the months following the adoption of the strategy, the technical secretariat of the Inter-Ministerial Committee for the Promotion of Foreign Investment will be charged to develop sector-specific Action Plans that will detail co-ordination and collaboration arrangements among the various line ministries.

Similarly, the strategy does not provide details on the monitoring and evaluation (M&E) framework that will be used to track its implementation. InvestChile is given a broad mandate to monitor and evaluate the investment promotion activities included in the prospective action plans on an annual basis. However, such a mandate should be accompanied with the necessary organisational, monitoring and data collection frameworks as well as sufficient resources to ensure that the strategy remains effective. InvestChile should be supported in developing a comprehensive internal M&E framework that will allow them to track and collect reliable statistical data based on international standards.

Setting the strategy in motion will require increased attention on the issues of policy alignment and co-ordination as well as the use of robust monitoring tools to identify policy inefficiencies and take corrective action. The Action Plans that will be developed by InvestChile in the first months of 2023 should create an integrated vision across government and set out long-term strategic objectives, quantifiable targets, programme actions and clearly defined roles for all the institutions involved in their implementation. They should include a detailed description of communication channels and co-ordination mechanisms as well as a set of quantifiable performance indicators that allow the tracking of investment promotion activities and the collection of data on their impact.

In this context, InvestChile's co-ordinating role could be strengthened through the agency's participation in high-level government councils that focus on sustainable development. Currently, InvestChile is a member of the Inter-Ministerial Committee for Foreign Investment and the National Council for Green Hydrogen (Figure 3.6). Participating in the activities of other councils such as the ones dealing with productivity, innovation, sustainability and skills development could help foster greater synergies between these policy areas and Chile's investment promotion priorities.

Overall, improving the inclusiveness of high-level government councils could become a priority to help address challenges in co-ordination. For instance, in January 2023, the Ministry of Economy established an Inter-Ministerial Committee for Sustainable Productive Development to co-ordinate policy efforts aimed at the diversification of the economy, without however InvestChile and the Ministry of Foreign Affairs, in particular SUBREI, being part of it. Given the importance of investment and trade policy in improving the productivity and accelerating the diversification of the Chilean economy, ensuring their involvement in the committee's deliberations and policy initiatives will be of paramount importance. Effective horizontal co-ordination across ministries and agencies will require clear and strong decision-making processes and high-level political commitment – i.e. at the ministerial and presidential levels – to overcome potential policy siloes, mobilise public resources and government actors, and build momentum behind the sustainable investment policy agenda.

Figure 3.6. Institutions at the intersection of investment promotion and sustainable development

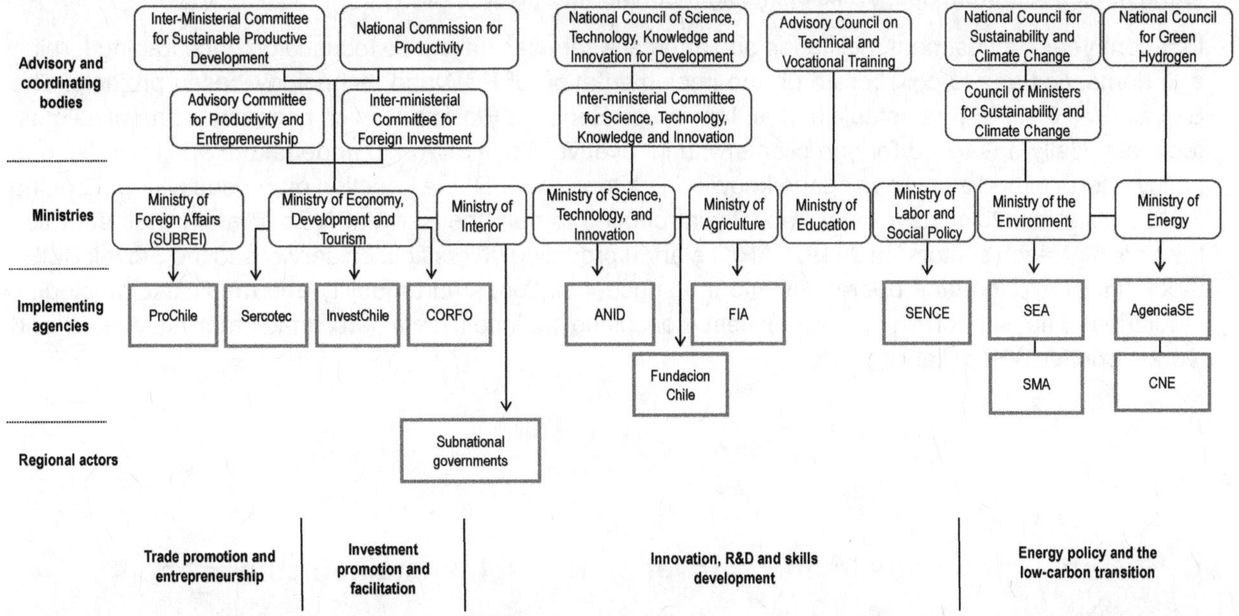

Note: SERCOTEC: National Service for Technical Co-operation; CORFO: Chilean Economic Development Agency; ANID: National Agency for Research and Development; FIA: Foundation for Agricultural Innovation; SENCE: National Service for Training and Employment; SEA: Environmental Assessment Service; SMA: Environmental Superintendency; AgenciaSE: Energy Sustainability Agency; CNE: National Energy Commission.
Source: OECD elaboration.

Box 3.3. FDI and economic diversification policies delivered by the Slovak IPA

The Slovak Republic shows a high level of economic specialisation. Most of the country's value added and employment, are concentrated in a few sectors, mainly in the automotive industry, and a number of low-tech sectors, such as wholesale and retail trade, real estate activities and construction. Although the motor vehicles industry alone is responsible for 20% of total manufacturing value added, foreign affiliates operating in the automotive industry are involved in low value-added activities (fabrication and assembly of imported car components). Their investment generates, therefore, scarce local technology diffusion, which hampers the sector's and the overall economy's potential to upgrade to more knowledge-intensive activities.

Recent policy reforms in the Slovak Republic have focused on diversifying the economy beyond low value-added manufacturing and strengthening its innovation potential. The Regional Investment Aid Scheme is the main instrument used by the Slovak Government to support investments that help the economy move away from low value-added manufacturing and towards more knowledge-intensive and high-tech sectors. The scheme provides aid in the form of grants for tangible and intangible fixed assets, corporate income tax relief, wage subsidies for newly created jobs and discounts in the renting or selling of real estate. The sectoral scope of the Regional Investment Aid Scheme illustrates the government's strategic choice to support FDI-intensive sectors to move higher up the value chain and engage in technologically sophisticated activities with more local content in their products. To benefit from the aid, investment projects should fall under one of the defined investment categories, namely industrial production, technological centres and business services centres, each one of which is linked to priority sectors (e.g. chemicals, electronics, automotive, business services etc.) and relevant smart industry technologies (e.g. robotics, artificial intelligence, big data, cloud, etc.).

In recent years, investment facilitation and aftercare services have also focused on encouraging foreign and domestic firms to collaborate on the implementation of R&D and technology-based projects. The Slovak IPA, SARIO, has established an Innovation Services Platform, which connects some of its most technologically advanced foreign clients with innovative Slovak firms to undertake R&D. In addition to policy efforts aimed at increasing the knowledge intensity of FDI (see section on productivity-enhancing FDI), similar initiatives have been recently introduced to help the Slovak SMEs diversify their activities towards high-tech sectors. In 2019, SARIO started providing diversification services to the Slovak SMEs that want to expand their operations into the space, aviation, smart mobility and medical technologies industries. The support includes business-consulting services, seminars, matchmaking events and workshops for B2B collaboration.

Source: OECD (2022[19])

3.4. Boosting productivity and innovation through sustainable investment promotion

3.4.1. Financial support for business R&D and innovation is among the lowest in the OECD area

Chile is placed among OECD and partner economies that provide one of the lowest levels of total government support for business R&D, at a rate equivalent to 0.03% of GDP in 2018 (latest available data (Figure 3.7). The Chilean support to business R&D – both direct (e.g. grants, loans) and indirect (e.g. tax relief) – ranks far from top innovators such as the US, Canada, France and Portugal.

R&D tax incentives account for the smallest share of public support to business R&D (28%) (OECD, 2021[20]). A tax incentive for extramural R&D was first introduced in 2008, whereby enterprises operating in Chile are entitled to a 35% tax credit for R&D certified contracts entered into with a registered research centre. The scheme is jointly administered by the Chilean Internal Revenue Service (IRS) and the Chilean Economic Development Agency (CORFO). The latter is also responsible for approving the registration of local research centres and certifying their R&D contracts agreed with business enterprises. The generosity of the tax incentive increased significantly in 2013 with the extension of the scope of R&D tax support to additionally cover intramural R&D and the ceiling on qualifying R&D expenditure was lifted from UTM 5 000 to 15000.

The magnitude of tax support, while small by international standards (in absolute and relative terms) has increased significantly over the past decade, ranging from USD 47 million in 2008 to USD 15 382 million in 2018. This was also reflected in the number of recipients, which increased in Chile, from less than 5 in 2008 to around 50 recipients in 2019 (OECD, 2021[20]). Unlike other OECD economies, this increase is primarily driven by large firms, which accounted for 73% of recipients and 92% of R&D tax support, while SMEs accounted for only 27% and 8% respectively. Although there are no disaggregated data on the basis of firm ownership to distinguish between domestic and foreign-owned firms, these findings are a sign that the scheme likely has a strong uptake among knowledge-intensive foreign MNEs, which are often large firms operating in the manufacturing and services sectors.

Figure 3.7. Chile's government support to business R&D is among the lowest in the OECD area

Percentage of GDP

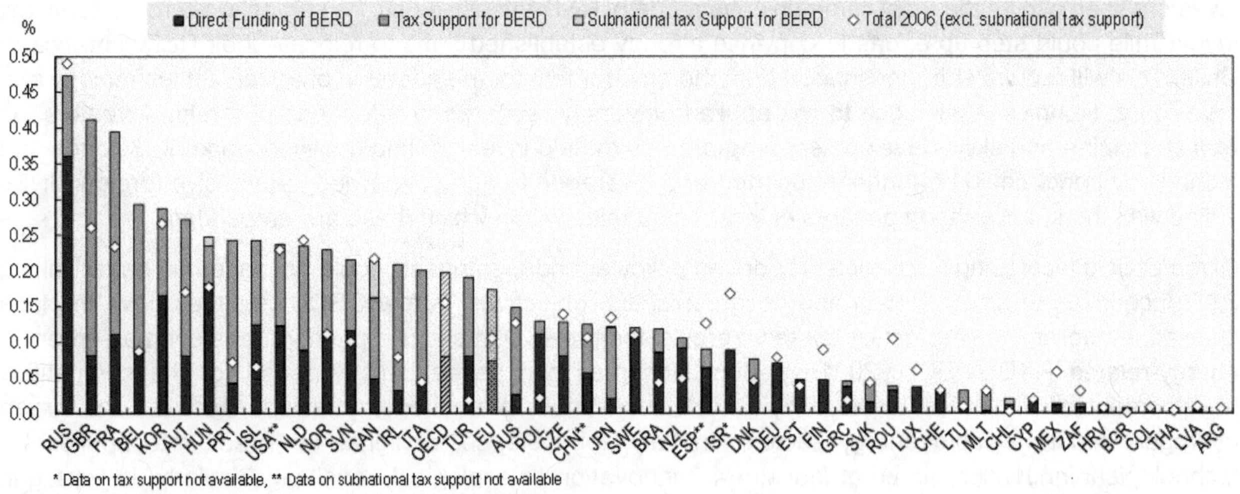

Source: OECD R&D Tax Incentive Database, (2021[21]), http://oe.cd/rdtax

However, the overall low level of R&D government support could be a barrier to attracting additional investment in R&D-intensive activities, in particular given that certain LAC countries may provide more generous schemes (e.g. Brazil, Colombia). Cross-country differences in the generosity of R&D tax allowances can lead to differences in the cost of capital faced by foreign MNEs – and subsequently encourage or discourage them from increasing their R&D investment or locating their R&D functions in a country.

The low uptake of R&D tax relief by Chilean SMEs may also be a sign of weak domestic capacities in the area of innovation, which could be an important barrier for domestic enterprises to develop value chain linkages and technology-intensive partnerships with foreign MNEs operating in Chile. This is unlike other OECD economies. Overall, SMEs represent at least 70% of tax relief recipients in 24 out of 30 countries included in the OECD R&D Tax Incentives Database, ranging from around 70% in Japan and 90% in the Netherlands to 100% in Denmark and New Zealand.

Potential reporting and other compliance constraints may limit the scheme's overall effectiveness in incentivising R&D collaborations. For instance, a pre-approval process is required to obtain the incentive and only expenses associated with pre-approved R&D projects are eligible for tax relief (EY, 2022[22]). In addition, the registration of research centres with CORFO comes with several requirements such as proving that they have the necessary organisational and material means and human resources to perform R&D, operating for at least six months and proving that they have sufficient financial reporting mechanisms to manage R&D projects. In many cases, delays in the certification of R&D expenditures by CORFO have led to the need to rectify tax declaration ex-post, adding administrative burden on firms that choose to claim the tax relief (OECD, 2022[3]).

Chile could consider adjusting the current scheme to make it more attractive and less burdensome for both foreign and domestic firms who seek to engage in innovative activities (e.g. simplifying application procedures, increasing the scheme's ceilings), while at the same time monitoring the scheme's impact and evaluating whether its benefits outweigh potential costs (e.g. in terms of forgone public revenue, economic distortions, etc.). Such reforms should be accompanied by measures to remedy a lack of awareness of the tax credit among smaller enterprises and other R&D institutions that operate in FDI-intensive sectors.

Certain OECD countries offer preferential provisions for SMEs and loss-making firms, and others provide comprehensive investment incentive packages that go beyond tax relief and seek to encourage the establishment of R&D and technology centres by foreign MNEs (e.g. Slovak Republic, see Box 3.3). Incentives are not the only policy tool to boost R&D investment, putting aside the question of their effectiveness and the forgone revenues they can generate. In many cases, the expansion of existing investors seems to be the most common entry mode of R&D-intensive FDI. As part of its aftercare services, InvestChile could step up efforts to convince already established firms to relocate their R&D activities to Chile. This will require stronger support from the government for the adoption of advanced technology and machinery, technical assistance to link applied university research to the needs of foreign investors, as well as training and skills development programmes to help investors find qualified workers. Science and technology parks could be further supported and leveraged to attract knowledge-intensive foreign MNEs in line with the specialisation patterns of local economies within which these are embedded.

Given Chile's increasingly sustainability-driven policy agenda, emphasis could be placed on better linking R&D incentives to green growth and decarbonisation objectives. A few OECD countries have in place special, temporary or emergency tax relief provisions for R&D in specific priority areas such as green or energy-related R&D (OECD, 2021[23]). Such schemes can be particularly useful for the competitive development of industries targeted by Chile's investment promotion framework, such as the green hydrogen and renewable energy sectors. In Italy, for instance, a higher tax credit rate applies for technological innovation aimed at industry 4.0 innovation or ecological transition. Similarly, in Portugal, relief for expenses related to the making of eco-design products is increased by ten after approval by the Portuguese Environment Agency.

3.4.2. Streamlining and scaling up Chile's investment incentives framework could help attract technology-intensive and low-carbon investments

Direct government funding in the form of grants and loans could be also increased and better co-ordinated and targeted in order to promote Chile's strategic priorities in the area of sustainable development and economic diversification. Direct funding often represents a more discretionary and selective form of public support as it allows governments to target specific economic activities that are considered to offer high social returns – as opposed to tax incentives, which are in principle available to all firms carrying out R&D.

In Chile, financial support for innovative and productive investments is offered by several public institutions. CORFO, under the supervision of the Ministry of Economy, Development and Tourism, offers more than 50 programmes and financial instruments aimed at promoting innovation, stimulating entrepreneurship, and strengthening the competitiveness of the Chilean economy (Table 3.2). In recent years, the focus of the agency has shifted towards financing national and foreign investment projects in sectors and value chains of strategic importance for Chile's economic transformation. For instance, since 2020, CORFO has launched several financing calls inviting domestic and foreign firms to benefit from preferential prices on Chile's lithium production for the manufacturing of lithium-based products (e.g. batteries). Similar financing schemes have recently been launched for the agricultural and green hydrogen industries.

Like CORFO, the National Agency for Research and Development (ANID), which reports to the Ministry of Science, Technology, Knowledge and Innovation, offers a wide range of short-term funding tenders as well as technical assistance programmes focusing on the promotion of both basic and applied research in all areas of knowledge, technological development and scientific innovation. Finally, the Foundation for Agricultural Innovation (FIA), under the supervision of the Ministry for Agriculture, provides support for the implementation of innovation initiatives in the forestry and agricultural sector and the associated agro-food chain through financing, seed capital, training and consulting services.

Table 3.2. Main investment incentives offered by Chilean Government institutions

Incentive scheme	Description
CORFO's Investment and Working Capital Guarantees	Intended to improve the access and funding conditions for companies developing an investment project or requiring working capital. Guarantees are granted to lending institutions by CORFO.
VAT exemption	Projects that involve an investment of at least USD 5 million can apply for a tax credit with regards to capital goods imported.
Tax credits and grants for investments in remote areas	Tax credit and grants for projects in Chile's northernmost regions of Arica – Parinacota & Tarapacá, as well as the southernmost Chilean zones of Palena Province (Los Lagos Region), Aysén and Magallanes (Chilean Patagonia). A special subsidy is also granted for productive investments by small and medium-sized investors.
Free trade zones	Free trade zones are defined physical places located in the Arica y Parinacota, Tarapacá and Magallanes regions, where goods are exempt from customs duties and taxes.
CORFO's Programme for Integrated Development Initiatives	Support for the materialisation of investment projects or expansion of existing technological investments, which generate impact in relevant productive or geographical sectors, by virtue of its alignment with the strategic axes of CORFO.

Source: OECD based on InvestChile (2022[24]), https://investchile.gob.cl/programs-and-incentives-for-investment/

Despite the multiplicity of government actors involved in supporting innovative and R&D-intensive investment projects, Chile's current institutional arrangements, funding mechanisms and policy mix lack an overarching framework that could identify strategic opportunities across sectors and provide the necessary long-term finance to diversify the country's production structure and hasten its transition towards a knowledge-based economy. The current financing model, which consists of a variety of calls and funding tenders with different requisites, objectives and timeframes, and implemented by various sectoral ministries and government agencies, does not provide the necessary long-term perspective in practice, which is particularly important for foreign firms when they consider where to locate their investments.

Given the need to catalyse additional investment for productivity growth and innovation, the Government of Chile is currently considering ways to streamline and consolidate its financial incentives framework. One option would be to leverage the potential of the new Inter-Ministerial Committee for Sustainable Productive Development to co-ordinate the administration and granting of the various incentive schemes in a more coherent way. Another option would be for the government to leverage the potential of CORFO, or a new development bank or the already established Banco del Estado, a state-owned bank which has been providing financial solutions to consumers and businesses, in particular SMEs, since 1955. The aim should be to make available a diverse portfolio of funding tools (e.g. loans, grants, guarantees, equity investments) and network-building initiatives to crowd-in private investors, including foreign MNEs, through risk-sharing, co-financing strategies and public-private partnerships (OECD, 2019[25]).

The relevance of such alternative financial options for sustainable investment promotion in Chile stems from the need to mobilise additional foreign investment through risk mitigation tools and approaches. The experience of other OECD economies suggests that direct financial support for the competitive development of strategic sectors should be transparent, time-limited and address well-identified market failures in order to avoid potential market distortions (OECD, 2022[1]). The conditions and criteria for granting financial support should be clearly defined and rules-based to avoid discretionary and distortive granting decisions. The activities should be also evaluated periodically to ensure that the benefits outweigh potential costs.

It will be important that the consolidation of the incentives framework relies on clear strategies, policies and targets that align available funding tools with Chile's investment promotion, innovation and low-carbon priorities. Such alignment can be achieved through the participation of key government agencies such as InvestChile, CORFO and ProChile in the management and coordination of the new framework. In Portugal, for instance, the national IPA is one of the shareholders of the National Promotional Bank, together with the Portuguese entrepreneurship and tourism promotion agencies (Box 3.4). The bank has been given a broad mandate to support investments in areas such as business financing, innovation funding, green finance, social cohesion and infrastructure development.

Box 3.4. Promoting innovation and the low-carbon transition through a national promotional bank: the case of Portugal

The ease of financing and promoting innovation has been a longstanding issue in Portugal. In 2020, the Portuguese Government established a National Promotional Bank (Banco Português de Fomento, BPF) to support SMEs, midcaps as well as large companies considered important for the development of strategic sectors of the Portuguese economy, by means of targeted funding, equity, and hybrid instruments and guarantees. BPF is a fully state-owned bank and its shareholders include: (i) the Portuguese State; (ii) the Agency for Competitiveness and Innovation (IAPMEI); (iii) the National Tourism Agency (Turismo de Portugal); and (iv) the Agency for Investment and Foreign Trade (AICEP Portugal Global). The participation of key government agencies in BPF's corporate governance structure as shareholders facilitates co-ordination and allows for greater synergies across the investment promotion, innovation and entrepreneurship policy agendas. At the same time, it acts as a bridge between the different needs and priorities of foreign and domestic firms, and expands credit supply for innovative, technology-intensive and low-carbon investment projects.

BPF has been given a broad mandate to ensure that its financing instruments support investments that contribute to sustainable development objectives. The bank's activities focus on five key areas of the Portuguese economy:

- Business financing: particularly SMEs and mid-caps, but also large corporations under certain conditions.
- Innovation funding: projects related to digital transformation, connectivity, entrepreneurship and R&D
- Green finance: investments related to sustainable infrastructures, transport, carbon neutrality, and the circular economy
- Social impact: health care, education, social housing
- Infrastructure: national and local infrastructure development projects in collaboration with local actors

Source: OECD (2022[14])

3.4.3. Strengthening knowledge and technology spillovers from FDI will require greater collaboration between InvestChile, Sercotec and CORFO

Business linkages between foreign investors and domestic firms, in particular small and medium-sized enterprises (SMEs), can be an important channel for the transfer of technology, knowledge and skills. Business linkages can take many forms. They may involve buyer-supplier arrangements along local value chains or formal strategic partnerships such as joint ventures, contract manufacturing, and R&D collaboration.

InvestChile does not implement any FDI-SME linkages programmes and does not operate a suppliers database, which is a common tool used by IPAs to support foreign MNEs' local sourcing strategies. They do, however, organise bilateral meetings between their clients and representatives of local business ecosystems to exchange information on potential opportunities for collaboration. InvestChile could consider complementing its portfolio of services with an online suppliers database and the organisation of regular matchmaking events and business fairs in sectors of strategic importance for the Chilean economy. Efforts to strengthen FDI-SME linkages will require sufficient resources and dedicated staff that is trained to identify the sourcing needs of foreign investors and steer FDI projects towards locations with the greatest potential for supporting supplier linkages.

For the implementation of these initiatives, synergies could be developed with CORFO, which supports many large domestic companies, and Sercotec, which supports Chilean SMEs through technical assistance, funding for innovative and export-oriented activities, and entrepreneurial training programmes. Sercotec also provides financial support to groups of companies to collaborate, establish business associations and participate in international business fairs. Although the support offered to Chilean SMEs is comprehensive, its scope is not always sufficiently aligned with the needs of foreign investors and the country's investment promotion priorities. This is also reflected in the limited co-ordination and collaboration that currently exists between InvestChile and Sercotec. To harness FDI-SME linkages, supplier development programmes should be aligned with the priorities and objectives of investment promotion and facilitation (e.g. in terms of sectors, activities and types of firms targeted) and combined with other types of support such as capacity building for local firms, training programmes for local staff, and cluster development initiatives. Knowledge and technology spillovers from FDI-SME linkages cannot materialise unless Chilean SMEs have sufficient absorptive capacities and can become successful suppliers and partners of foreign investors.

The Supplier Clubs programme, which is implemented jointly by the Portuguese IPA (AICEP) and SME agency (IAPMEI) is a good example of how public policy can mobilise actors across the business ecosystem to help local SMEs collaborate with foreign MNEs. The programme combines matchmaking services to help foreign and domestic firms identify collaboration opportunities and agree on jointly implemented projects; business consulting services and training programmes provided by foreign affiliates to their suppliers based on an assessment of the latter's performance; and financial support through EU-funded incentive schemes to help SMEs upgrade their technological capabilities for the implementation of the agreed joint projects. Such a systematic approach to value chain building in Chile will require the use of a more diverse range of policy instruments and greater co-ordination among the agencies involved in investment promotion and SME growth policies. InvestChile could consider collaborating with CORFO and Sercotec for the implementation of a supply chain development programme, involving investors and domestic firms, including SMEs, supported by the three agencies.

3.5. Promoting skill-intensive investment and addressing skill gaps in FDI-intensive sectors

3.5.1. Labour market regulations may discourage foreign MNEs from investing in training

Labour market regulations can support foreign firms' adjustments while providing a level of employment stability that encourages learning in the workplace. Balanced labour market rules matter for the location choice of foreign investors and affect FDI volumes – and thus potential job creation – as well as their knowledge intensity (Javorcik and Spatareanu, 2005[26]). But job security also protects workers from being fired in response to small fluctuations, which can encourage foreign MNEs to invest in long-term training. In Chile, restrictions to individual and collective dismissals of regular workers are relatively strict and slightly above the OECD average (OECD, 2019[27]). Rules for hiring workers with temporary contracts are less strict but still above many other OECD countries.

As seen in many OECD economies (e.g. Portugal, the Netherlands, Sweden) relatively low regulation of temporary contracts in situations of high regulation of regular contracts can deter employers from offering permanent employment opportunities to workers. This labour market duality results in Chile having one of the highest shares of temporary jobs and a high job turnover (OECD, 2020[28]). In 2021, Chile ranked fourth among OECD economies in terms of the share of workers on temporary employment (26.5%), and far above the OECD average of 11.8% (Figure 3.8). Among LAC economies, Chile also has the highest share (48%) of workers with one year or less of job tenure, followed by Peru and Colombia. Short job tenure and low costs of dismissal severely affect foreign and domestic firms' incentive to invest in job training.

Employment protection reforms can reduce labour market duality between secure and precarious jobs by lowering the opportunities and incentives for firms to replace regular with temporary contracts. In the case of Chile, this would involve reforms that restrict the valid cases for use of temporary employment. In Portugal, for instance, the 2019 labour market reform reduced the maximum duration of temporary contracts from three to two years and introduced a requirement for firms to justify their use (OECD, 2022[14]). The Contrato-Geração incentive scheme was also implemented with the aim to promote permanent employment for both first-time jobseekers and the long-term unemployed.

As seen in Chapter 2, foreign MNEs in Chile create more skill-intensive jobs than domestic firms. However, opportunities for human capital development could still be further leveraged by diversifying the type of FDI that Chile has attracted so far, mainly in medium- and low-tech manufacturing, mining and construction. Reducing the complexity of regulatory procedures, in particular for large investment projects, in high-tech and knowledge-intensive activities (e.g. business services) would support FDI to create better paid and more high-skilled jobs. FDI impacts on jobs and skills are also likely to be greater in settings where pro-competition policies allow for more efficient resource reallocation. Perceptions of the private sector suggest that several key markets in Chile are dominated by relatively few firms, making Chile the 39th most concentrated economy out of 141 (OECD, 2022[3]; WEF, 2019[29]).

Figure 3.8. High employee turnover limits incentives for firms to invest in training

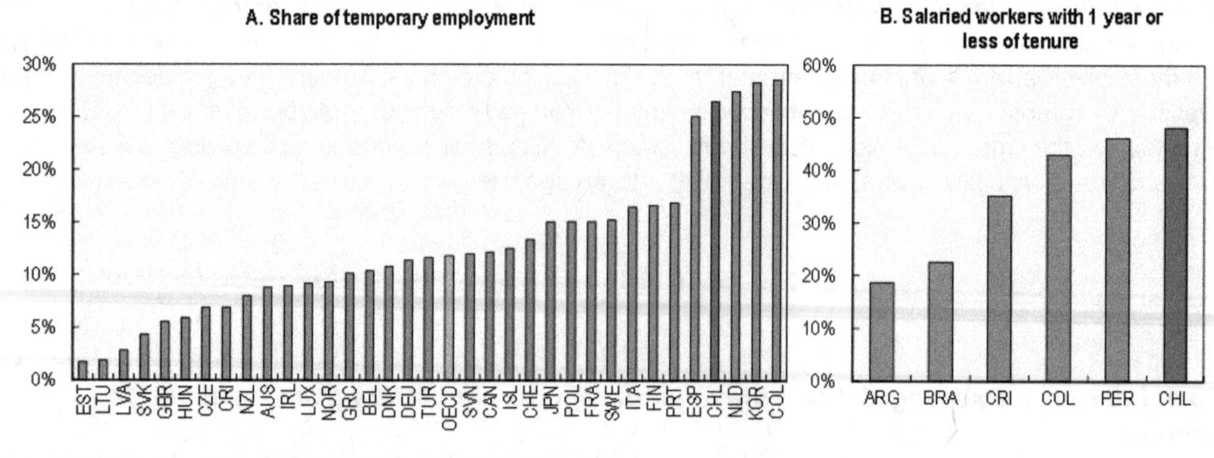

Note: Data in Panel A refer to 2021. Data in Panel B refer to 2019.
Source: OECD labour force statistics (OECD, 2023[30]), https://doi.org/10.1787/23083387, and IADB Sims Database (IADB, 2022[31]), https://mydata.iadb.org/en/Labor/Database-of-Labor-Markets-and-Social-Security-Info/v2c9-36h7

The government has sought to incentivise on-the-job training through a tax franchise scheme, which allows foreign and domestic firms to benefit from tax credits (up to 1% of their wage costs from their tax liability) if their workers participate in training courses offered by the National Training and Employment Service (SENCE). The latter supervises and promotes a wide variety of upskilling and reskilling initiatives and supports the employability of workers, whether they are employed or not. However, evidence from multiple evaluations suggests that government-funded training programmes face challenges in matching the supply and demand of jobs, have high dropout rates and poor results in terms of addressing skill gaps in strategic sectors of the Chilean economy (Bogliaccini et al., 2022[30]). The number of workers benefitting from the tax franchise scheme has been following a downward trend over the past decade while there is little involvement of employers on the type of training that their workers get. An important root cause of these problems relates to the fragmentation of the institutional framework governing skills development as well as the lack of effective skill anticipation systems that take into account MNEs' changing needs with regard to workforce skills (see next section).

Investment promotion and incentive policies have a crucial role to play in supporting skills development. Foreign MNEs operating in Chile should be further incentivised to undertake training activities for their own employees or for their local suppliers. For instance, Thailand's investment incentive scheme includes a set of merit-based incentives that provide an add-on to the basic scheme with additional tax exemptions if a project undertakes R&D and skills development activities or locates in specific regions or in an industrial area (OECD, 2021[31]). Financial incentives targeting large investments, particularly those administered by CORFO and having a sectoral focus, could be aligned with these performance criteria. Such eligibility conditions require careful monitoring to ensure that the outcome has been met and to avoid fraudulent behaviour. The experience of Chile's tax franchise scheme suggests that training incentives should be flexible enough to allow foreign MNEs to tailor programmes to the needs of their employees. For instance, IDA Ireland has partnered with Skillnet Ireland, the Irish public agency responsible for skills development, to facilitate foreign investors' access to Skillnet's talent development programmes and provide them with tailored coaching and mentoring to assess their talent needs (Box 3.5). Sometimes, foreign MNEs create their own training centres, and many IPAs support them by ensuring that trainings are recognised by the relevant authority. Better co-ordination and collaboration between InvestChile and SENCE will be key to improve FDI's contribution to job training opportunities.

Box 3.5. Tailored skills development programmes for foreign investors in Ireland

In 2022, Ireland's investment promotion and skills development agencies, IDA Ireland and Skillnet Ireland respectively, launched a strategic talent development partnership. The partnership aims to supporting FDI companies who are looking to attract and retain talent by offering them access to tailored skill development initiatives implemented across Skillnet Ireland's 73 networks nationwide. This new engagement model combines the IDA's business development and support services for foreign MNEs with Skillnet Ireland's talent development expertise and extensive delivery network to help drive companies' growth.

Before the official launch of the partnership, the two agencies successfully piloted the programme by helping a selected number of foreign MNEs put together a strategic training and development plan to meet their business objectives. The programme involved coaching and mentoring to help companies assess their talent needs. External consultants were also assigned to work with them and help them address skill gaps and identify strengths and opportunities for further improvement. By the end of 2022, more than 20 companies have gone through the programme in a wide range of different sectors such as financial services, biopharmaceuticals, aviation communications, manufacturing and software development.

Skillnet Ireland has previously teamed up with IDA Ireland and Technological University Dublin to develop its Transform programme, an accredited course designed to help companies equip their staff with automation and tech skills. The programme has had notable success for Dell Technologies in supporting the company to enhance the talent capacity of 600 members of its Ireland-based workforce and has resulted in the development of 190 business innovation projects. In 2021, Skillnet invested EUR 1m to bring the programme to a wider network of businesses in Ireland. This supports businesses – large and small – in their adoption of digital transformation and propels their workforce to embrace digitisation as it applies to leadership, strategic business models and advancing human digital capital capabilities.

Source: OECD based on IDA Ireland (2022[32])

3.5.2. Skills development incentives and programmes should be better linked to foreign MNEs' changing needs

Chile's plan to become a value-based, innovation-driven economy, and to attract investment accordingly, is only possible if the skills gap and mismatch are addressed quickly. Most importantly, ensuring that everyone has the right skills for an economy increasingly driven by sustainability considerations and the digital transformation is essential to promote inclusive labour markets, spur innovation, productivity and growth.

In Chile, responsibility for the formulation of skill development policies is shared among the Ministry of Education, the Ministry of Economy and the Ministry of Labour. Government agencies under their supervision are responsible for implementing a variety of reskilling and upskilling initiatives. The National Agency for R&D (ANID) implements the Becas Chile Scholarships programme, which supports Chilean students to pursue postgraduate studies at high-quality universities and enhance their research, technology and innovation skills. CORFO is also financing the training and certification of workers in programming and ICT skills. The agency's human capital scholarships support workers in various productive sectors and geographic areas of the country through professional specialisation courses.

Many programmes also aim to improve institutional capacities. For instance, CORFO's New Engineering 2030 programme helps universities that teach civil engineering to transform their institutional practices, training and links with industry and society, and contribute to the productive development of the economy through innovation, entrepreneurship and technology transfer. Sectoral programmes are also implemented. The Foundation for Agricultural Innovation (FIA) seeks to develop knowledge, skills and attitudes around the cycle of innovation and entrepreneurship in youth, adults, professionals, technicians and entrepreneurs linked to the forestry and agricultural sector and/or the country's agri-food chain.

Despite the number of skills development programmes offered by the various government agencies, evidence suggests that training programmes are not always of good quality, face challenges in targeting their objective population and are insufficiently aligned with the needs of the labour market (Larrañaga, 2011[33]; OECD, 2018[7]). Recent ILO research has found that in Chile there is an overall lack in demand for training, and, when it occurs, training benefits mostly highly educated workers (e.g. senior professionals) or workers in occupations with high demand for specific skills (Bogliaccini et al., 2022[30]). Training programmes in Chile should mutually strengthen the skills of the highly and less educated in order to address the challenges that digitalisation and the low-carbon transition – all accelerated by FDI – impose on the labour market. They should also better target job seekers and vulnerable groups of workers, including women and unemployed, who may be adversely affected by foreign MNEs' changing needs or FDI's diversification away from natural resources sectors. To this end, sectoral retraining programmes can be more impactful than general training courses, as they reduce skills shortages in target sectors where FDI may crowd out competitors unable to retain their talented staff.

The government has realised the benefits of opening the labour market to highly skilled non-Chileans, particularly for knowledge-intensive activities. Chile has modernised its immigration regulations offering a clear regulatory framework to promote and facilitate the movement of natural persons for business purposes. Through the recently approved Law No. 21,325, on Migration and Foreigners and Decrees No. 296 and No. 177, the country has established certain mechanisms to facilitate the process of granting visas for foreigners who intend to settle in Chile for a limited period and develop activities related to the business world. Despite this, 19 commercial agreements have assumed commitments in the movement of business people, establishing different categories in which the investor is incorporated.

Although facilitating labour mobility across all sectors could help address skill gaps across the entire economy, the government should ensure that FDI-intensive sectors and sectors with significant skills gaps remain a priority. Robust monitoring mechanisms to track the evolution of skill shortages could allow the government to quickly identify gaps and prioritise those sectors that need international talent the most. InvestChile could play an important role in that respect by liaising with the National Migration Service to address potential excessive delays in the granting of visas for its clients and help them find the skills they need. Policies to attract higher-end foreign investments should mechanically result in attracting highly skilled foreigners to work in the promoted projects.

If Chile wants to diversify into high-tech and knowledge-intensive activities, including by attracting more FDI in these sectors, it needs to invest in a broader set of skills, beyond those required in sectors where FDI is already present (i.e. natural resources, finance, low-tech manufacturing). This will require robust skills anticipation systems that involve the investment community and allow to design evidence-based and forward-looking programmes that match expected skills needs in various industrial sectors (e.g. data science, artificial intelligence, cloud computing). The Advisory Council on Technical and Vocational Training (an entity headed by the Ministry of Education in collaboration with other ministries, agencies, educational institutions and some business associations) could play a more active role in the implementation of skills needs assessments and in the collection of information on foreign firms' operations and skills needs. Involving InvestChile in the council's activities and foresight exercises could help better reflect the skills needs driven by FDI.

On the investment promotion side, InvestChile could also further promote sectors or activities in alignment with the existing skills base and provide appropriate information to investors on labour market characteristics. Currently, the agency does not provide any services to help foreign investors identify local workers with relevant skills. Recently, however, it has collaborated with CORFO and Fundacion Chile, a public-private innovation agency, to support foreign MNEs that had reinvestment processes paused due to a lack of skilled workforce. The programme seeks to train 1 000 workers according to the specific requirements of their companies, enabling a potential investment of USD 80 million and an increase of approximately USD 20 million in services exports.

Moving forward, InvestChile should co-ordinate with SENCE, CORFO and Chile's labour intermediation offices for the development of joint programmes and initiatives that allow foreign MNEs to find the skills they need. Costa Rica's IPA, CINDE, helped create an online platform, "The Talent Place", that provides detailed up-to-date information regarding in-demand occupations, skills required to apply and links to resources to obtain need certification (Box 3.6). SENCE already operates the Geo-SENCE platform, which geographically visualises skills distributions and needs, as well as training and company-employee matching opportunities throughout Chile. Further synergies could be built between skills development and investment promotion initiatives to ensure that InvestChile's clients have tailored access to CORFO and SENCE's existing information services.

Box 3.6. Costa Rica's framework for linking FDI to labour market outcomes

Costa Rica is one country in which the IPA, CINDE, plays a particularly significant role in skills, through partnerships, studies and advocacy. Education and human talent is one of CINDE's identified strategic pillars. According to the IPA's 2019-22 strategy, the agency identifies itself as a key player in supporting skills development for jobs of the future, and in the transitioning towards a knowledge economy. CINDE is fulfilling the strategy to boosting skills in Costa Rica in partnership with ministries, other agencies, universities, technical institutions and the foreign MNEs themselves, allowing the IPA to closely track patterns in emerging human talent Among other objectives, it aims to strengthen the links between the enterprises it attracts and the local economy and improve the level of skills and labour market outcomes of the local population through several programmes:

- CINDE helped create an online platform, "The Talent Place" (www.thetalentplace.cr) that provides detailed up-to-date information regarding most in-demand occupations, current vacancies in the companies located in Costa Rica, skills required to apply and links to resources to build them and obtain needed certification, including though free-of-charge online courses. Aiming at directly linking employers with employees, CINDE also organises, on an annual basis, the "CINDE Job Fair" (www.cindejobfair.com) which matches available vacancies in MNEs that were supported by CINDE with potential job seekers. During the 15 years of the fair's operation, 10 000 people assisted the fair, 24% of which have completed the recruitment process.
- Together with the Ministry for Science, Technology and Telecommunications and "Essential Costa Rica", responsible for the country brand, CINDE has also designed a programme for innovation and human capital development (Programa de Innovación y Capital Humano, PINN). The initiative provides Costa Rican nationals with access to scholarships funding educational opportunities in science, technology, engineering and mathematics (STEM). The programme is supported by the Inter-American Development Bank, and CINDE serves as a certification and capacity-building body under one of its pillars.
- CINDE also contributes to an overall understanding of the labour market and education outlook of Costa Rica, including skills needs, which encourages programmes that further boost the country's attractiveness as an FDI destination. One of these programs was launched in September 2021, Technological Seedlings, in which CINDE has partnered with Microsoft to boost the talent pool in certain high-tech sectors identified in CINDE's studies as needing the most new entrants. The training of these students has been relegated to the INA, Costa Rica's primary agency for learning and skills development, showing a strategic positioning of an IPA to actively shape skills development at home.
- In light the COVID-19 crisis, in April 2020, CINDE also created an online platform that offers information on job vacancies available in MNEs located in the country. The goal has also been to facilitate a transfer of employees from sectors most affected by the pandemic (e.g. tourism) to other sectors that have remained relatively intact as well as more generally support worker mobility. As of April 2020, 950 jobs were on offer on the platform.

Source: OECD (2021[31])

3.6. Harnessing the potential of FDI for green growth and the low-carbon transition

3.6.1. Promoting green FDI will require reforms in carbon pricing and incentives for further renewable energy expansion

Creating an enabling environment for green and low-carbon investment has been an important and longstanding policy priority for the Government of. The key institutions responsible for developing, implementing and financing proactive policies and programmes to decarbonise the economy are the Ministry of Energy and the Ministry of the Environment. However, other sectoral ministries and government agencies such as the Ministry of Mining, the Ministry of Economy, CORFO and InvestChile are also involved in efforts to decarbonise the economy. An Inter-ministerial committee and a national council on sustainability and climate change have been established to assess the environmental impact of economic activities and foster co-ordination and synergies among the public and private sectors.

Recent initiatives have focused on setting low-carbon transition targets and long-term policy strategies that send investors, including foreign ones, strong signals regarding the government's climate ambitions. Chile is the first Latin American country that made emission targets legally binding through its 2022 Framework Law on Climate Change. The law establishes the requirement to develop a national multi-sector climate strategy that will define specific measures to achieve carbon neutrality emissions and sets out sectoral reduction targets that should be achieved through action plans developed by the respective sectoral ministries. It also defines specific policy instruments to achieve these objectives, including the development of a climate financing strategy by the Ministry of Finance and a law that defines greenhouse gas emissions limits and creates a transfer system when emission surpluses are detected.

In agreement with the coal-fired plant owners and operators, the government has put forward a decarbonisation plan for the electricity system, which aims to phase out or reconvert all coal-fired power plants by 2040 (IEA, 2021[34]). The first phase, planned to be completed by 2024, will decommission 11 out of the 28 coal-fired units that are currently concentrated in six communes across Chile. Such clear and long-term targets are critically important to build capacity for investors to understand transition risks and to attract foreign investment that contributes to the country's climate agenda.

Mobilising low-carbon FDI to support Chile's climate ambitions will require strong co-ordination for the implementation of targeted policies, in particular for hard-to-abate sectors and industries for which FDI could significantly contribute to their decarbonisation. Currently, energy is responsible for 52% of greenhouse emissions in Chile, followed by the transport sector with 25% (OECD, 2022[3]). Over the past decade the contribution of fossil fuels to electricity generation has declined while wind and solar energy have gained traction. Renewable sources produce 47% of electricity; however, coal is still used to generate one-third of total electricity, significantly above the OECD average. These findings suggest that, despite progress, Chile still heavily relies on carbon energies due to the weight of the transport sector and the growth in the energy-intensive needs of certain industries (e.g. mining). There is room for the energy, electricity generation and transport sectors to further contribute to the country's low-carbon transition.

Chile has been a regional leader in attracting FDI in renewables over the past decade (see Chapter 2). An important feature of the Chilean renewable market development is the absence of investment support mechanisms or direct public subsidies, tax benefits or feed-in tariffs. Instead, the Government of Chile has relied on mandatory quotas; auctions that allow renewable energy generators to have power purchase agreements with distribution companies; and recently a system of net metering allowing consumers to produce their electricity from renewable energy sources (Bersalli, 2019[35]). Clean energy projects are exempted from paying tolls for using the main electrical transmission system (InvestChile, 2021[36]). Measures were also taken to facilitate the connection of the electrical system to renewable energy plants of smaller capacity and guarantee their access to distribution facilities. Challenges regarding access to land for renewables investment are also being addressed. Between 2018 and 2021, the Ministry of National Assets tendered 136 plots of land for energy investment, all of them located in Chile's northern regions (InvestChile, 2021[36]).

Chile's current long-term goals of 100% zero-emission electricity generation and 80% renewable energy by 2050 will require to keep a fast pace of investment in clean energy. Achieving this target may require the government to put forward additional policy instruments in the future. For instance, feed-in tariffs are a type of incentive designed specifically to accelerate investment in renewable energy technologies by offering long-term contracts to renewable energy producers (OECD, 2022[1]). They reduce the risk of renewable energy investments by guaranteeing a predetermined price (or revenue) for the electricity generated for a predefined period of time. Studies have found evidence that feed-in-tariffs are a powerful tool for attracting FDI in renewables, both in advanced and developing countries (Wall et al., 2018[37]). For carbon and energy-intensive activities in the mining and industrial sectors, in which many foreign MNEs are concentrated, incentives for the deployment and use of renewable energy could be another option. Guaranteed access to networks, priority dispatch, tax credits and soft loans could accelerate the energy transition in these industries (Simsek et al., 2019[38]).

Carbon pricing is also a core climate policy instrument that provides a technology-neutral case for low-carbon investment and consumption. While carbon pricing policies do not specifically target FDI, they are a necessary first step to send the socially optimal price signals to all investors, including foreign ones, and raise the returns on low-carbon relative to high-carbon investments. In 2017, Chile introduced a set of taxes on emissions of pollutants and a tax for new vehicles. However, the level of carbon taxes is significantly low compared to international standards and their coverage is limited. In 2021, carbon taxes in Chile covered 33.2% of greenhouse gas emissions, while fuel excise taxes, an implicit form of carbon pricing, covered 22.6% of emissions, unchanged since 2018 (OECD, 2022[39]). The tax level of USD 5 per ton of CO2 emitted is also far from the commonly used benchmark of EUR 60 per ton (OECD, 2022[3]). The 2022 OECD Economic Survey of Chile provides a set of recommendations to improve the effectiveness of the carbon pricing framework (Box 3.7), focusing in particular on streamlining aspects related to the level and coverage of carbon taxes as well as co-ordinating their implementation with industry.

In terms of regulation, market access restrictions in the transport sector, a major CO2 pollutant, (Figure 3.2) could be lifted to help Chile meet its net-zero emission targets. Current restrictions on FDI are likely to result in sub-optimal flows of investment, limit the transfer of know-how and may hamper the deployment of low-carbon technologies. The Government of Chile has introduced a requirement that only zero-emission vehicles can be sold after 2035, including light vehicles, public transport and machinery, including mining trucks. Opening up the sector to technology-intensive foreign MNEs will be necessary for the electrification of the vehicle fleet.

Box 3.7. OECD recommendations to reform Chile's carbon pricing framework

The 2022 OECD Economic Survey of Chile has found that the limited impact of Chile's carbon tax scheme may be related not only to its low level, but also its limited coverage. The review proposes the following recommendations:

- The current level of the carbon tax limits abatement efforts. Higher carbon prices are crucial to accelerate the transition towards sustainable energy sources.
- Future policy initiatives should establish a gradual timeline towards higher levels of the carbon tax and wider implementation of cap-and-trade systems. The latter will allow power plants to exchange permits through trade and auctions.
- The scheme's coverage could be improved by considering accelerated exemptions for power plants using renewable energy sources from the carbon tax.
- The establishment of a climate advisory board, as done in the UK for example, or of other institutionalised channels for climate policy dialogue could help improve the industry's acceptance of higher carbon prices.

Source: OECD (2022[3]), OECD Economic Surveys: Chile 2022, https://doi.org/10.1787/311ec37e-en.

3.6.2. Chile's emerging green hydrogen industry will require investment and capacity building across the entire value chain

The Government of Chile has made its priority to create an enabling framework for attracting investment in the green hydrogen industry. A national strategy was adopted in 2021 setting ambitious targets for the development of the industry, including for Chile to produce the cheapest hydrogen in the world by 2030 and to be among the world's three largest exporters by 2040 (Ministry of Energy, 2020[40]). Specific measures have been identified to speed up green hydrogen use in the domestic market and identify opportunities for future exports. Measures include a USD 50 million round of finance for green hydrogen projects to create an early demonstration experience for potential investors (CORFO, 2021[41]). At the end of 2021, CORFO approved six project proposals for the establishment of production plants that are expected to enter operation by 2025 and attract investments of USD 1 billion. The strategic framework was complemented with the adoption of a 2023-30 Action Plan which defines the roadmap for the sustainable development of the industry, focusing on clarifying the institutional framework, developing the local value chain for green hydrogen production, and strengthening the necessary infrastructure and territorial readiness.

If the Government of Chile decides to pursue the development of the green hydrogen industry, uncertainties about the demand for green hydrogen versus other energy-related sources and technologies, which are currently more cost-competitive, should be taken into consideration since they are a key obstacle for mobilising private capital. In addition, given the early technological maturity of hydrogen technologies and the high risks involved, regulatory reforms across the value chain and targeted public policy interventions will be necessary to create the conditions for private investment. As was the case with the deployment of wind and solar energy generation facilities over the past decade, achieving industry growth will require a trained workforce, pursuing parallel demonstration projects, the use of public-private partnerships and financial incentives to derisk production costs and create certainty for investors.

For the initial phase, time-limited financial support schemes could reduce the investment risk for the industry and close part of the cost differential with other types of energy sources. The establishment of new financial tools, as mentioned in the previous section, could help in the deployment of grants, concessional loans and guarantees to make investment projects more bankable (IEA, 2021[42]). The Australian Government, for instance, has put forward an investment package for new energy technologies, including for hydrogen for which more than USD 1.26 billion have been pledged (IRENA, 2020[43]). The Australian Energy Agency (ARENA) currently implements a grant programme aimed at demonstrating the technical and commercial viability of hydrogen production, and the Clean Energy Finance Corporation, Australia's government-owned green bank, will make more than USD 200 million available to support the hydrogen industry. In the case of Chile, such a specialised financial institution could also support feasibility studies to identify near-term opportunities, and provide technical assistance and capacity building for the initial deployment of key technologies.

Scaling up low-carbon hydrogen and use will require timely investments in enabling infrastructure, including new transmission lines (for low-carbon electricity to reach the electrolysers for on-grid projects), hydrogen transport and storage infrastructure and port terminals (IEA, 2021[42]). Incentives for investments in value chain segments that support the production of green hydrogen solutions should be also considered, e.g. for the manufacturing of equipment such as electrolysers and fuel cells, that could help reduce production costs but also create highly qualified jobs and economic opportunities for regional economies. Given the segmentation of the value chain, it is important that investment incentives for green hydrogen target locations that already have facilities for renewable energy production so that inter-related value chain segments can be better integrated.

While FDI can play a strategic role in sustainable energy supply and green hydrogen manufacturing, scaling up private investment in green hydrogen will not be possible without addressing demand-side bottlenecks. Demand for green hydrogen could be promoted through phase-out mandates, similar to those implemented in fossil fuel or nuclear power – for instance by phasing out blast furnaces for steel or fossil fuel-based ships and replacing them with green hydrogen-powered components (IRENA, 2020[43]). Legally binding mandates and quotas are also alternative options to create a market for green hydrogen and other renewable energy sources (e.g. solar and wind energy), for instance by requiring a share of gas demand to be met by renewables or specifying a share of renewables in existing uses and for specific applications. In the EU, France has already mandated the use of 10% of low-carbon hydrogen in industry by 2023, which is meant to go up to 40% by 2028.

Chile's mining industry, which is dominated by foreign MNEs and continues to receive significant FDI, could use green hydrogen as well as electricity from solar and wind energy to displace large volumes of diesel and enable significant emissions reductions in the long term. The mining sector is one of the largest emitters of greenhouse gas in Chile, and about 30% of electricity is used to extract and process raw materials (Ministry of Energy, 2021[44]). Foreign mining companies operating in Chile, like Collahuasi for instance, have already announced their plans to replace current diesel-powered haul trucks with hydrogen-powered technology. The Government of Chile has recently launched the National Mining Policy 2050 that sets ambitious targets for the low-carbon transition of the mining sector, including zero-emission fleet plans for all large-scale mining operations by 2025 (Ministry of Mining, 2022[45]). Setting these targets is a step in the right direction; however, achieving carbon neutrality in the mining sector will also require consultation with the industry to assess the feasibility of the transition plans as well as technical co-operation with foreign MNEs and public-private partnerships to resolve potential regulatory bottlenecks in the deployment of the green hydrogen technology. Portugal's Sectoral Pacts for Competitiveness and Internationalisation represent a good example of how such collaboration among various sectoral stakeholders could take place, by integrating clear-cut targets, a diverse range of support instruments – including reforms to the regulatory environment – and a robust monitoring and evaluation framework to ensure the alignment of policy initiatives with regional and sectoral needs (Box 3.8).

Box 3.8. Fostering public-private partnerships: the mineral resources cluster in Portugal

Since 2017, the Portuguese SME Competitiveness and Innovation Agency, IAPMEI, has recognised 18 industrial clusters (*clusters de competitividade*) in Portugal with the aim to foster greater collaboration among government agencies, domestic and foreign companies, business associations, universities and other non-corporate entities of the Portuguese research and innovation ecosystem. Since their establishment, the clusters have played a crucial role in supporting foreign MNEs and Portuguese SMEs to implement smart specialisation strategies, identify bottlenecks in the industry's performance, and provide feedback to government on the implementation of regulatory reforms and business support programmes. Financial support to recognised clusters is provided through the Portugal 2020 Incentives Scheme, which includes a dedicated set of financial instruments for collective actions, networks and other forms of business-to-business and science-to-business partnerships.

In 2019, "Sectoral Pacts for Competitiveness and Internationalisation" were signed between the Ministry of Economy and Digital Transition and some of the recognised clusters. The Pacts provide a framework to strengthen the innovation and internationalisation of industrial clusters through joint public-private sector initiatives, including: measures that promote industry 4.0 practices; industry-led training and skills development programmes; innovation activities; actions to promote the brand and strengthen the attractiveness of Portuguese clusters; and targeted reforms in the regulatory environment to address barriers to innovation and internationalisation in specific sectors and value chains. A Monitoring Committee was also set up to ensure the implementation of the agreements.

The Mineral Resources Cluster

In 2019, the Mineral Resources Cluster was among the clusters that signed a Sectoral Pact with the Ministry of Economy and Digital Transition, setting out several objectives for the internationalisation of the minerals sector and specific measures to achieve them. These include:

- *Produce knowledge and induce innovation in the sector* – Measures: i) Create an online platform with information about mineral resources; ii) Implement an innovation programme for Portugal's lithium resources; iii) Conduct a study to support mineral exploration; iv) Establish an integrated system to assess the potential use of abandoned flooded quarries as water reserves; v) Support the digital transformation of the industry's business models, processes and products; vi) Conduct a study to assess the potential of marine mineral resources in the continental shelf.
- *Promote the creation of value and identify opportunities for exports* – Measures: i) Strengthen the internationalisation of the cluster; ii) Support companies that aim to initiate export processes; iii) Promote international brands; iv) Create a Centre of Intelligence and Technology for Natural Stone.
- *Promote efficiency and sustainability in the use of mineral resources* – Measures: i) Implement an integrated mining plan in the Marble Zone; ii) Establish a Green Agenda for Mineral Resources; iii) Conduct a study on the environmental liabilities of mineral raw materials.
- *Promote skills and social responsibility practices* – Measures: i) Promote training programmes on digitalisation, circular economy, occupational health and other skills related to extraction activities; ii) Promote the "Social License" concept; iii) Bring young people closer to the industry.
- *Increase the visibility of the sector* – Measures: i) Strengthen networking with international clusters; ii) Open specific tenders for the implementation of cluster strategies; iii) Foster greater synergies with IAPMEI.

Source: IAPMEI (2021[46])

References

Agosin, M. (2009), "Se justifica una política industrial hacia la inversión extranjera? El Programa de Atracción de Inversiones de Alta Tecnología", *Trabajos de Investigación en Políticas Públicas, Universidad de Chile*. [16]

Bersalli, G. (2019), *Chile, an emerging key actor in the renewable energy arena*, http://www.climate-chance.org/wp-content/uploads/2019/12/cp2-2019-energy-chile_en_20191204.pdf. [37]

Bogliaccini, J. et al. (2022), *(Un)Employment and skills formation in Chile: An exploration of the effects of training in labour market transitions*. [32]

CORFO (2021), *First call for the financing of Green Hydrogen Projects in Chile*, http://www.corfo.cl/sites/Satellite?blobcol=urldata&blobkey=id&blobtable=MungoBlobs&blobwhere=1475168300448&ssbinary=true. [43]

de Crombrugghe, A. and S. Moore (2021), *Investment promotion and the digital economy: a comparative analysis of investment promotion practices across the OECD*, http://www.oecd.org/daf/inv/investment-policy/Investment-Insights-Investment-Promotion-Digital-Economy-OECD.pdf. [5]

EY (2022), *Worldwide R&D Incentives Reference Guide*, https://assets.ey.com/content/dam/ey-sites/ey-com/en_gl/topics/tax/tax-guides/2022/ey-worldwide-r-and-d-incentives-guide-2022.pdf. [22]

Government of Canada (2019), *Canada-Chile Free Trade Agreement*, http://www.international.gc.ca/trade-commerce/trade-agreements-accords-commerciaux/agr-acc/chile-chili/index.aspx?lang=eng&_ga=2.211116501.1706717867.1561574602-1846205196.1561057909. [9]

Government of Chile (2023), *Agenda de Productividad*, http://www.hacienda.cl/noticias-y-eventos/presentaciones/agenda-de-productividad. [4]

IADB (2022), *Database of Labor Markets and Social Security Information System (SIMS)*, https://mydata.iadb.org/en/Labor/Database-of-Labor-Markets-and-Social-Security-Info/v2c9-36h7. [31]

IAPMEI (2021), *Clusters de Competitividade: Pactos para a competitividade e internacionalização*, http://www.iapmei.pt/getattachment/PRODUTOS-E-SERVICOS/Empreendedorismo-Inovacao/Eficiencia-Coletiva-e-Clusters/BrochuraClusters04052021.pdf.aspx. [48]

IDA Ireland (2022), *IDA Ireland and Skillnet Ireland announce strategic talent development partnership*, http://www.idaireland.com/latest-news/press-release/ida-ireland-and-skillnet-ireland-announce-strategic-talent-development-partnership. [34]

IEA (2021), *Decarbonization plan for the electrical system*, International Energy Agency, http://www.iea.org/policies/12978-decarbonization-plan-for-the-electrical-system. [36]

IEA (2021), *Hydrogen in Latin America: From near-term opportunities to large-scale deployment*, OECD Publishing, Paris, https://doi.org/10.1787/68467068-en. [44]

InvestChile (2022), *Chapter II: Investment Incentives*, https://investchile.gob.cl/programs-and-incentives-for-investment/. [24]

InvestChile (2022), *Foreign Investment in Chile in 2021*, https://investchile.gob.cl/wp-content/uploads/2022/03/reporte-ied-en-chile-a-marzo2022.pdf. [13]

InvestChile (2021), *Energy: Projection and Opportunities*, https://investchile.gob.cl/wp-content/uploads/2021/04/03ebook-energia-eng-.pdf?_ga=2.232923994.552586033.1668452665-1099269533.1668037335. [38]

IRENA (2020), *Green Hydrogen Cost Reduction: Scaling up Electrolysers to Meet the 1.5ºC Climate Goal*. [45]

Javorcik, B. and M. Spatareanu (2005), "Do foreign investors care about labor market regulations?", *Review of World Economics*, Vol. 141(3), pp. 375-403. [26]

Larrañaga, O. (2011), *Informe Final, Comisión Revisora Del Sistema de Capacitación e Intermediación Laboral, report of a commission of experts of the Ministry of Labour and Social Welfare*, http://www.cl.undp.org/content/chile/es/home/library/poverty/informes_de_comisiones/informe-final-comision-revisora-del-sistema-de-capacitacion-e-in.html. [35]

Ministry of Energy (2021), *Se crea 1° Red de Eficiencia Energética y Reducción de Emisiones en la Minería*, https://energia.gob.cl/noticias/nacional/se-crea-1deg-red-de-eficiencia-energetica-y-reduccion-de-emisiones-en-la-mineria. [46]

Ministry of Energy (2020), *National Green Hydrogen Strategy*, https://energia.gob.cl/sites/default/files/national_green_hydrogen_strategy_-_chile.pdf. [42]

Ministry of Mining (2022), *National Mining Policy 2050*, http://www.politicanacionalminera.cl/wp-content/uploads/2022/03/MINING_2050_NATIONAL_MINING_POLICY.pdf. [47]

Nelson, R. (2007), "Transnational Strategic Networks and Policymaking in Chile: CORFO's High Technology Investment Promotion Program", *Latin American Politics and Society*, Vol. 49/2, pp. 149-181, https://doi.org/10.1111/j.1548-2456.2007.tb00410.x. [17]

OECD (2023), *OECD Labour Force Statistics 2022*, OECD Publishing, Paris, https://doi.org/10.1787/dc0c92f0-en. [30]

OECD (2022), *FDI Qualities Policy Toolkit*, OECD Publishing, Paris, https://doi.org/10.1787/7ba74100-en. [1]

OECD (2022), *OECD Economic Surveys: Chile 2022*, OECD Publishing, Paris, https://doi.org/10.1787/311ec37e-en. [3]

OECD (2022), *Pricing Greenhouse Gas Emissions - Key findings for Chile*, OECD Publishing, Paris, http://www.oecd.org/tax/tax-policy/carbon-pricing-chile.pdf. [41]

OECD (2022), *Strengthening FDI and SME Linkages in Portugal*, OECD Publishing, Paris, https://doi.org/10.1787/d718823d-en. [14]

OECD (2022), *Strengthening FDI and SME Linkages in the Slovak Republic*, OECD Publishing, https://doi.org/10.1787/972046f5-en. [19]

OECD (2021), *OECD Economic Surveys: Chile 2021*, OECD Publishing, Paris, https://doi.org/10.1787/79b39420-en. [49]

OECD (2021), *OECD Investment Policy Reviews: Thailand*, OECD Investment Policy Reviews, OECD Publishing, Paris, https://doi.org/10.1787/c4eeee1c-en. [33]

OECD (2021), *OECD R&D Tax Incentive Database*, http://oe.cd/rdtax. [21]

OECD (2021), *OECD R&D Tax Incentives Database, 2021 edition*, OECD Publishing, Paris, http://www.oecd.org/sti/rd-tax-stats-database.pdf. [23]

OECD (2021), *R&D Tax Incentives: Chile, 2021*, OECD Publishing, Paris, http://www.oecd.org/sti/rd-tax-stats-chile.pdf. [20]

OECD (2020), *OECD Employment Outlook 2020: Worker Security and the COVID-19 Crisis*, OECD Publishing, Paris, https://doi.org/10.1787/1686c758-en. [28]

OECD (2020), *OECD FDI Regulatory Restrictiveness Index*, http://www.oecd.org/investment/fdiindex.htm. [2]

OECD (2019), *OECD Indicators of Employment Protection*, OECD Publishing, Paris, http://www.oecd.org/employment/emp/oecdindicatorsofemploymentprotection.htm. [27]

OECD (2019), "Scaling up climate-compatible infrastructure: Insights from national development banks in Brazil and South Africa", *OECD Environment Policy Papers*, No. 18, OECD Publishing, Paris, https://doi.org/10.1787/12456ee6-en. [25]

OECD (2018), *Mapping of Investment Promotion Agencies in OECD Countries*, OECD Publishing, Paris, http://www.oecd.org/investment/Mapping-of-Investment-Promotion-Agencies-in-OECD-Countries.pdf. [18]

OECD (2018), *OECD Economic Surveys: Chile 2018*, OECD Publishing, Paris, https://doi.org/10.1787/eco_surveys-chl-2018-en. [7]

OECD (2018), *OECD Indicators of Product Market Regulation*, http://www.oecd.org/economy/reform/indicators-of-product-market-regulation/. [6]

OECD (2015), *Strengthening Chile's Investment Promotion Strategy*, OECD Publishing, Paris, http://www.oecd.org/daf/inv/investment-policy/Chile-investment-promotion-strategy-2015.pdf. [12]

Simsek, Y. et al. (2019), "Review and assessment of energy policy developments in Chile", *Energy Policy*, Vol. 127, pp. 87-101, https://doi.org/10.1016/j.enpol.2018.11.058. [40]

SUBREI (2022), *Current economic-commercial agreements*. [11]

SUBREI (2022), *Current international investment agreements*. [8]

SUBREI (2021), *Bases para la Estrategia de de Exportación de Servicios de Chile: Capitalizando las Ventajas Competitivas para Impulsar las Exportaciones de Servicios*, http://www.subrei.gob.cl/docs/default-source/estudios-y-documentos/otros-documentos/bases-para-una-estrategia-de-exportacion-de-serviciosb6198c5848864ed9a7c32b0a6c878acf.pdf?sfvrsn=91c7b2b8_1. [50]

Sztajerowska, M. and C. Volpe Martincus (2021), *Together or apart: investment promotion agencies' prioritisation and monitoring and evaluation for sustainable investment promotion*, http://www.oecd.org/daf/inv/investment-policy/Investment-Insights-Investment-Promotion-Prioritisation-OECD.pdf. [15]

Wall, R. et al. (2018), "Which policy instruments attract foreign direct investments in renewable energy?", *Climate Policy*, Vol. 19/1, pp. 59-72, https://doi.org/10.1080/14693062.2018.1467826. [39]

WEF (2019), *Global Competitiveness Report 2019*, http://www.weforum.org/reports/how-to-end-a-decade-of-lost-productivity-growth. [29]

WTI (2022), *Sustainable Development in Chilean International Investment Agreements*, World Trade Institute, http://www.wti.org/media/filer_public/d3/96/d3967dfa-0393-42bf-a3e9-cb519943562e/wti_working_paper_07_2022_sustainable_development_in_chilean_international_investment_agreements.pdf. [10]

www.ingramcontent.com/pod-product-compliance
Lightning Source LLC
LaVergne TN
LVHW060454061126
851857LV00016B/1819
9789264329881